Beethoven and Me

A Beginner's Guide to Classical Music

BEETHOVEN AND ME

A Beginner's Guide to Classical Music

by

Earl Ofari Hutchinson

MIDDLE PASSAGE PRESS

Beethoven and Me: A Beginner's Guide to Classical Music

www.classicalmusicforbeginners.com

Printed in the United States

Published by
Middle Passage Press
5517 Secrest Drive
Los Angeles, California 90043

Designed by Alan Bell

Publisher's Cataloging-in-Publication
(Provided by Quality Books, Inc.)
Hutchinson, Earl Ofari.
Beethoven and me : a beginner's guide to classical music /
by Earl Ofari Hutchinson.
pages. cm.
Includes bibliographical references and index.
ISBN 978-0692508176
1. Music appreciation.
2. Music—History and criticism.
I. Title.
MT90.H88 2015
781.68
QBI15-600092

Table of Contents

"There is no theory.

You merely have to listen.

Pleasure is the law."

—Claude Debussey

Preface

Writing a first time book on Western Classical Music was both an intense labor of love and a challenge. For decades I have inhabited another world that seemingly is as far removed from the day's political and social conflicts that I have specialized in discussing and writing about for years. At first glance, the world of classical music seems as distant from hard political commentary as the Galactic space between the sun and the moon. Yet, I managed over the years to bridge that space by writing and commenting on the music, the artists and the composers on my radio shows and in occasional columns.

During these years there were many persons who have nurtured my appreciation and understanding of classical music. This is my opportunity to thank those who have been of invaluable aid and support.

They include: Dr. Carolyn Sweeney, Professor, Music Department West Los Angeles College, Dr. Janise White, Professor, Music Department, West Los Angeles College and Founder, Afro-American Chamber Music Society, Priscilla Pawlicki, Pasadena Conservatory of Music, Lisa White and Lisa Bellamore, Los Angeles Philharmonic, Don Lee White,

Founder, DLW Chorale,. Leslie Leighton, Assistant Conductor, the Los Angeles Master Chorale, Grant Gershon, Conductor, LAMC and Libby Huebner, publicist, LAMC and L.A. Chamber Orchestra.

I owe a deep debt of gratitude to Nikki Leigh, Charles Dickerson, Founder and Music Director, the Inner City Youth Orchestra, Los Angeles, Dr. Gwen Wyatt, the Gwen Wyatt Chorale, Geoffrey Pope, Assistant Conductor, UCLA Philharmonia Orchestra and Russell Steinberg, Founder and Music Director Los Angeles Youth Orchestra, and Neal Stulberg, Chairman, UCLA's Herb Alpert School of Music and Conductor of the UCLA Philharmonia Orchestra, and Leni Boorstin who provided priceless suggestions and corrections to the manuscript and press material.

I also must thank Alan Bell who did the superb layout and formatting of the book, Fanon Hutchinson who produced a superlative promotional video, Angela Hoffman who did the sterling cover photography, and Autumn Conley who spent long hours with the manuscript to insure total impeccable editorial quality and smooth reading flow.

I also received tremendous support from my close friends, supporters and family members, Sikivu Hutchinson, Dwayne Wyatt, Pedro Baez, Linda Hunt and Kathy Hutchinson who also offered invaluable suggestions and heartfelt support.

The last name on my thank you list is Barbara Hutchinson, my wife. Through all of my dozen books and publishing ventures spanning two decades, she has been a rock of support. She offered crucial tips and suggestions for this book as well as providing the index for it.

They are the ones who made it possible for me to boldly step out of my role as a political and social commentator and show that classical music and the compelling social issues of the day need not be separate. Again, I thank them for making *Beethoven and Me: A Beginner's Guide to Classical Music,* a reality.

Ludwig van Beethoven

INTRODUCTION

Beethoven and Me: A Beginner's Guide to Classical Music

The Seventh Symphony "is one of the happiest products of my poor talents."

—Beethoven

From My Concert Seat: The Curtain Opens

It started for me with Beethoven's *Seventh Symphony*. To be more precise, it started with that particular piece in a music appreciation class I took at Los Angeles City College (LACC) as a teenager in 1965. My father and uncle were professional musicians; respectively, they played the saxophone and clarinet. Both toured with bands in the Army and later in the Midwest. Nevertheless, other than one very short-lived effort at the seemingly obligatory piano lessons those musically and non-musically inclined parents impose on their children, I had no real musical inclination or facility. During my high school years in

the 1960s, my listening began and ended with the Temptations, Marvin Gaye, the Supremes, the Four Tops, and James Brown. If it wasn't R&B or pop and I couldn't dance to it, it basically didn't exist.

Looking back, I recall the instructor did not play the entire symphony. Rather, he stopped it in order to discuss the different parts. In rapid succession, he explained, "This is called the andante. This is called the allegro. This is called the scherzo. This is called the minuet. This is called the rondo. This is a note. This is a scale. This is a bar." Yes, I was supposed to be learning all of those terms, but they really didn't matter to me; they were meaningless. A few days earlier, if anyone would have asked, I would have said a scale is merely something to weigh oneself on and a bar is a place for one to get sloppy drunk. The terminology really meant nothing.

What did mean something—everything to me, in fact—was a plethora of things I had never really experienced before: the powerhouse sound; the flow; the melody; the rhythm; the obvious passion, energy, and excitement that exploded in my ear upon hearing that music. My first order of business was to get the Beethoven *Seventh*. I wanted to hear the entire work, unhindered and unimpeded by an instructor's explanation of what I was listening to. In the pre-*Amazon* era and even the pre-chain music store era, there were still independent record stores. I had never purchased a record; I just listened to the Motown and soul sounds on my small transistor radio and at high school dances. The Beethoven *Seventh* was my first authentic vinyl purchase.

The year 2015 marked exactly fifty years since that music appreciation class in 1965. During that half-century, I regularly programmed, featured, and promoted classical music on my radio shows on the Pacifica Radio Network. I have interviewed many conductors from the classical world, as well as composers, and performers. I have written extensively in my syndicated columns about classical musical developments. To this day, that passion ignited in 1965 still exists.

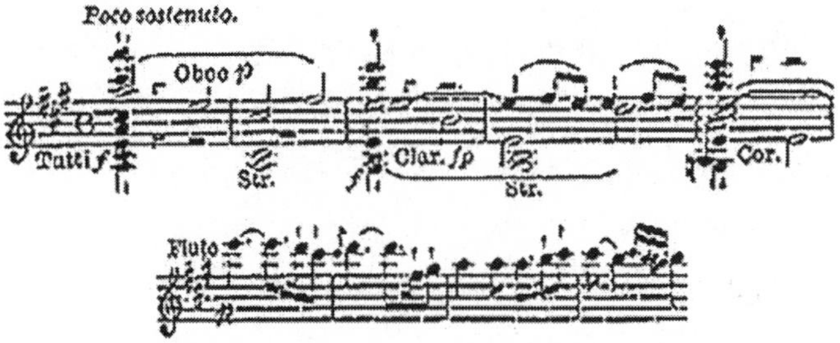

The opening and theme of the first movement of Symphony No. 7
Beethoven in 1814
by Louis-Rene Letronne

From My Concert Seat

In late July of 2013, I thought I'd surely died and gone to heaven. That week, I had the great privilege of attending the world-renowned Aspen Music Festival in Aspen, Colorado, an annual, month-long event that features an almost 'round-the-clock program of symphonies, cham-

ber works, master classes, and lectures on every aspect of classical music. I had the opportunity there to mingle with and interview musicians and the administrative staff of the festival, and that was a most unforgettable experience.

My biggest thrill, though, was watching and listening to the training orchestras as the expertly regaled us with some of the greatest classical works. They brought so much energy, passion, and just plain fun to the music that it was infectious. An added plus for me was that the orchestras resembled a mini-United Nations gathering. Among the very talented musicians were African-Americans, Hispanics, Asians, and Middle Easterners, and that made it obvious that the future of classical music is, in fact, in very good hands. By no means is it a dying art.

In the twenty-year period from 1995 to 2015, I attended nearly 500 concerts. Among the orchestras who have soothed my ears are the Israel Philharmonic, Armenian National Philharmonic, London Symphony, Berlin Philharmonic, San Francisco Symphony, Philadelphia, The Academy of St Martin in the Fields, the Rotterdam Philharmonic, the St. Petersburg Philharmonic, the New York Philharmonic, Utah Symphony, and Tafelmusik, to name a few. I have attended multiple concerts by the Los Angeles Philharmonic Orchestra, as well as every southern California orchestra and chorale.

I have also attended many festivals, including Aspen,

Carmel Bach, and the Ojai Festival. I have heard nearly every major work, in every style, countless times, from symphonies to string quartets to oratorios, operas, tone poems, and chamber works. I have heard nearly every major concert virtuoso on nearly every major instrument. These great performances were conducted by a virtual *Who's Who* of the world's greatest conductors, including Sir Simon Rattle, Herbert Blomstedt, Esa-Pekka Salonen, Nicholas McGegan, Matthias Bamert, Michael Tilson Thomas, Lorin Mazel, Zubin Mehta, Alan Gilbert, Andrew Manze, Simon Trpceski, Rafael Fruhbeck de Burgos, Gustavo Dudamel, Christoph Eschenbach, Andre Previn, and Leonard Slatkin. This gave me a listener's-eye view of their wildly different conducting styles, mannerisms, and, most importantly, their interaction with the orchestra and the audience.

Beethoven and Me: A Beginner's Guide to Classical Music focuses almost exclusively on the composers, their works, and the structure of those works. They are the brick and mortar of the classical music house. The reason for this is simple: I am not a musician, composer, critic, or musicologist. I make no claim to have the depth, training, expertise, or detailed technical craft that only comes from decades of musical study and training. I make absolutely no claim that this book is exhaustive, comprehensive, or definitive. It is, just as the title says, for *beginners,* this classical music lover's personal and very selective, impressionistic walk through the history, tradition, and experience of classical music.

I have included a bibliography of the many varied

books on classical music for those who are moved enough by *Beethoven and Me*—which I hope you will be—to want to read and know more. I have also listed many books on the composers and their works in my source notes. I have purposely avoided using technical terms, but where absolutely necessary, I have provided an easily understood mini-definition of key musical terms and forms in various sections throughout the book.

I am not a fan of Top Ten lists of the best or even my favorite classical music numbers, as I find it a bit self-serving and presumptuous and tantamount to engaging in a debate over whether Wilt Chamberlain or Michael Jordan is the all-time greatest basketball player. Assigning a "best" ranking to any great composer and his or her work would be nothing more than a meaningless exercise.

The opening of the second movement

That said, I wholeheartedly recommend works in the opening chapter "Overture: A Guide to My Favorite Classical Terms," as I consider these to be representative of eight common musical forms and ensembles in classical music. I have also provided a *YouTube* link for listening to them. In addition, throughout these pages, I have sprinkled the names of many of the best-known works for further listening. This will give you a feel for varied styles and forms of the music from different time periods.

In the "From My Concert Seat" sections, like the one below, you will find very personal recollections of my experiences and observations at concerts over the years.

From My Concert Seat

It's rare that I hear their works performed or see them on the conducting podium with any of the major orchestras, so I'll make a major departure from my straight timeline guide to the music of the well-known old masters. I'll integrate a discussion of the works of the three groups that have been shamefully ignored, shunned, marginalized, or maligned in far too many works on classical music. I did not want to shove them into chapters at the end of the book, for they deserve far more notice than a mere afterthought in the end matter, and placing them there would only perpetuate the notion that they are marginal at best and insignificant at worst in the history and evolution of Western classical music; nothing could be further from the truth.

These are the black, Hispanic, and female composers. In their own way, and often against towering obstacles, they made their own unique stamp on Western classical music. They wrote, performed, and conducted significant classical music works that span every classical music form: operas, symphonies, tone poems, oratorios,

sonata works, quartets, sacred masses, and concertos. In the Jazz Age of the 1920s and afterward, they had a major impact on classical music and still do.

In classical music, there is no right or wrong, black or white when it comes to the enjoyment of listening and feeling. The proof is that, at times, even the greatest composers, such as Tchaikovsky and Brahms or Wagner and Verdi, thought the other's work was worthless. The music of composers such as Bach, Beethoven, Florence Price, Brahms, Prokofiev, Carlos Chavez, Ricard Strauss, Igor Stravinsky, or even Mozart, has, at times, been denounced, dismissed, or ridiculed for being lightweight, superficial, ugly, abhorrent, or unworthy.

From My Concert Seat

Over the years, I have sometimes had the chance to wander backstage to meet a conductor or concertmaster before the start of a concert. It's always a bustle back there, with the musicians and principals feverishly doing their last-minute preparations before going onstage. This was the case backstage at the season finale concert of the New Mexico Philharmonic in April of 2015. The one difference that time was the concertmaster. He had just had a medal penned on him by the Polish Counsel in the U.S. We took pictures and later, when he turned to the audience before the start of the concert and displayed the award, I felt a special joy for him. Moments like that have

made the classical music experience very personal and even more rewarding for me.

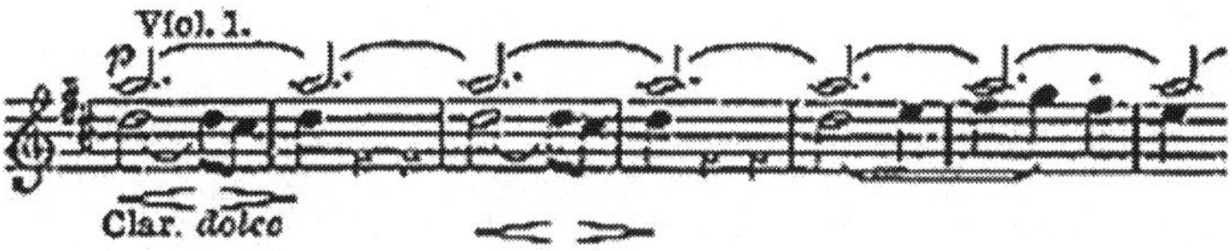

The scherzo and trio of the third movement

Encore

In the late 1990s, I was asked to moderate a panel tasked with examining the life and work of Russian great, Dimitri Shostakovich, at the Music Center in Los Angeles. The half-day event brought together some of the top local concert musicians, writers, critics, and composers. It was a freewheeling discussion, with no one point of view or interpretation of Shostakovich's music and how it played out against the colossal torment and repression he suffered for decades under the harsh thumb of Soviet tyrant Josef Stalin, shackled with composing under the rigid dictates of socialist realism in music. The only agreement the panel could come to was that Shostakovich, more often than not, produced truly profound music.

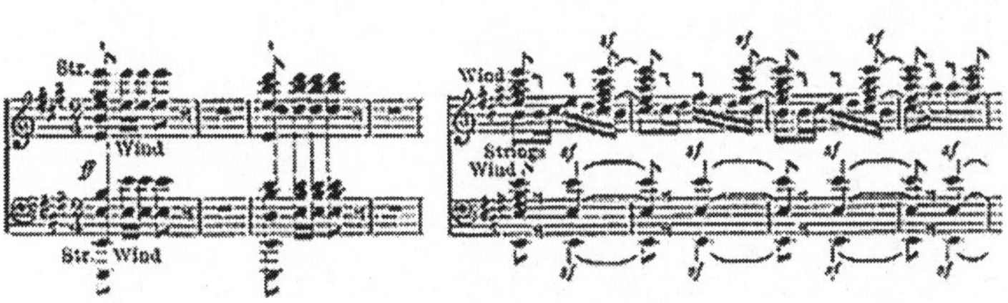

The opening and syncopated accompaniment of the finale

My goal with *Beethoven and Me: A Beginner's Guide to Classical Music* is to provide the beginning, casual, or novice listener of classical music with a memorable survey history of this music, from the Baroque to the modern period. The music discussed in these pages changed a teenager's life forever, and that teenager was me. I want to share that experience with you, for it may change your life as well.

OVERTURE

A Guide to My Favorite Classical Terms

"A symphony must be like the world.
It must embrace everything."
—Gustav Mahler

A guidebook that does not provide a traveler with points of reference for a trip isn't worth much. Thus, the aim of this overture is to provide you with a point of reference in my walk through the last 300 years of classical music. I'll start with a mini-look at my favorite forms, genres, and ensembles in the classical music world. I'll start with the small ones first.

The Sonata

You can't get more basic than this, as it is for a single instrument. It could be the piano, violin, oboe, cello, trumpet, or clarinet. In its smaller, simpler version, it's called a *sonatina*. Like so much of the terminology in classical music, *sonata* comes from the Italian for "sound," and this is not hard to remember when you hear one. The notes are arranged in a form that was more fully developed in the nineteenth century. It starts with a fast movement, then a slow one, and then a fast one at the end. But even this is not fixed. There might be only one or two movements to it.

Despite what some may think about classical music, most composers even long ago really did want their music to have a bit of swing to it. Otherwise, this fast-slow-fast sandwich would have been absolutely unnecessary.

From My Concert Seat

I have to confess that once, at a concert of the American Youth Symphony at UCLA's Royce Hall, I felt a sudden impulse to jump out of my seat and dance in the aisle to a particularly stirring rendition of Mozart's *Serenade No. 13 for Strings in G Major* (1787), more popularly known as *Eine Kleine Nachtmusik*. Fortunately, for me, sanity prevailed, but the compelling did make nonsense out of the notion that one can't dance to a classical music number. In fact, Beethoven—and especially Mozart—were quite the dancing duo. See my "Encore" to find out just how much of a duo they were when it came to the dance!

The well- and even lesser-known composers wrote legions of sonatas. More often than not, they wrote them to showcase their own prowess on their preferred instrument. The more they showcased themselves, the more concert bookings they got, and the more cash they raked in. Musician-composers have always been fans of creativity, but paying the bills is important too.

Recommended Listening

Bach's *Violin Sonata No.1 BWV 1001*
Itzhak Perlman, Violin
https://www.youtube.com/watch?v=etB8MAjNaz0

(Piano) Sonata Nº 1 - Op. 22 de Alberto Ginastera
Horacio Lavandera, Piano
https://www.youtube.com/watch?v=7-lcnVAoLRE

The Quartet

The sonata has to have some company. The company is an ensemble. It could be a trio of three instruments. But my favorite is the quartet ensemble and this is accomplished with four instruments together; most commonly, it consists of violins, a viola, and a cello, string instruments.

Such a string quartet is often employed by weddings and outdoor events. The form follows pretty close to that of its big brother, the symphony: fast, then slow, with a speedball ending. Usually, albeit not always, a string quartet plays four movements, sometimes including a *minuet* included. That was especially the case during the Baroque period, which we will discuss in more detail in the coming pages.

The minuet can be slow and stately. In dance form, it was all the rage with the European nobility of the seventeenth, eighteenth, and nineteenth centuries, who loved to dance into the night to the minuet at court shindigs. That adoration wasn't lost on composers; rather than just performing pieces to be listened to, they began creating music geared for moving one's feet.

I take great delight at concerts watching others in the audience sway their heads in time with the beat in those spiffy, sprightly, minuet-type sections of a quartet. Composers, though, didn't stop with four instruments. Since the violin, cello, and viola aren't the only things going on in an orchestra, they soon began writing quintets (five instruments), sextets (six instruments), septets (seven instruments), and octets (eight instruments). In fact, even very early on, some composer wrote numbers for many players. The form often stayed the same, only with more instruments.

Recommended Listening

Chevalier de Saint-George, *Quartet No.3 Op 14 in F Minor*
Apollon Quartet
https://www.youtube.com/watch?v=rOYJu_IWqhU

Dimtri Shostakovich, *String Quartet No. 8, in C Minor, Op. 110*
Kronos String Quartet
https://www.youtube.com/watch?v=3m5ohobcKb8

Encore

Mozart on *Dancing with the Stars*, Anyone?

I'm still trying to picture Mozart whirling around the dance floor. Yes, that's right: Wolfgang Amadeus himself, twirling and whirling and prancing around. He started dancing in public when he was five years old, in a Latin play *Sigismundus Rex,* staged in September of 1761. The play celebrated the end of the academic year in Salzburg, but Mozart didn't stop there. As an adult, he never missed a chance to show off his stuff on the dance floor. He even bragged about his twinkle toes once in a letter he wrote to his sister.

He doubled down on his eighteenth-century version of *Dancing with the Stars* routine by writing tons of dance music for balls, soirees, and other festive occasions, while on the payroll of Emperor Joseph II in the late 1780s; he held the title of the emperor's official royal and imperial chamber composer. Mozart kept very busy and wrote somewhere in the neighborhood of 500 dance numbers: minuets, German dances, country dances, you name it. Clearly, no one had to beg, "Rock me, Amadeus!" and he aimed to please.

Beethoven wasn't quite the dancing Harry Mozart was, but he didn't miss a chance to pen a few dance numbers himself. Often, one or another of his twelve *Contre-*

***danses,* written between 1791 and 1801, are played on classical music stations. A couple centuries before Duke Ellington uttered those timeless words, "If it ain't got that swing, it don't mean a thing," the dancing duo of Beethoven and Mozart took the Duke's immortal line to heart on the dance floor.**

The Oratorio

You don't have to be a church-, temple-, or mosque-goer to know this is a religious musical piece. Though there are non-religious oratorios, the best known were written for the church. In the early millennium of the evolution of classical music, the Catholic Church dominated every waking and breathing moment of people's lives in Europe. I was raised Catholic back in the day, so I know the feeling well. Mozart knew it well too. He set the fourteenth-century Eucharistic hymn in Latin *"Ave Verum Corpus"* to his *Ave Verum Corpus* as a motet to music. As a choirboy at Holy Cross Catholic School in Chicago, I sang this numerous times—in Latin, of course—at church festivals and special events. I still think I'm back in the choir at ol' Holy Cross every time I hear *Ave Verum Corpus,* and I hear it played a lot.

Composers in the pay of and at the beck and call of the Church wrote sacred pieces, motets, chants, and hymns. The oratorio was a natural step up from that, a big, sprawling work with chorus, soloists, and instrumental (later orchestra) accompaniment. The greatest of the great of the old masters—Bach, Haydn, Mozart, Beethoven, Mendelssohn and, of course, Handel—all wrote oratorios or sacred masses; yes, think *Messiah,* by Handel.

From My Concert Seat

I've made it part of my tradition for the past twenty years to never miss a local performance of Handel's *Messiah* during the Christmas season. I've heard it sung by major and local community choral groups, and no matter who does it, it always sounds pretty much the way Handel intended it, yet somehow fresh and new.

Recommended Listening

Felix Mendelssohn, *Elijah (Elias, Part I)*
Thomas Hampson, Barbara Bonney, Florence Quivar
Atlanta Symphony Orchestra & Chorus
https://www.youtube.com/watch?v=LlY8WQ5vLeY

Duke Ellington, *The Best of the Three Sacred Concerts*
Croatian Radio Television Jazz Orchestra and Choir
https://www.youtube.com/watch?v=ijr_ldvY-F8

The Overture

I always think of this when I think of opera; after all, that was how the overture got its start. Opera composers in the seventeenth century figured out that tossing in a brief, catchy, oftentimes rollicking number before or after the curtain rose was the perfect way to get the audience's attention and rev up the crowd. Giaochino Rossini (Italy, 1792-1868), before he found a new life as a very rotund gourmet chef in Paris after packing up his composing, was the absolute master of the opera and wrote thirty-nine of them. His overture to *William Tell* has been done to death in everything from movies, TV series like *The Lone Ranger,* and commercials.

From My Concert Seat

I grew up watching *The Lone Ranger* as a kid in the 1950s. When I've heard that familiar overture in concert, I still want to shout, "Hi, ho, Silver!" (though he actually said, "yo.") I guessed that by the looks on the faces of some of those sitting near me, who just so happened to be of my generation, they might have secretly been yelling that too.

It didn't take long for many overtures to become such fun listening that they became standalone pieces used to head up a concert bill. Some are so good that they have become well-established concert pieces played long after the operas they opened for, operas that were shoved into the dust bin and forgotten.

Recommended Listening

Wolfgang Amadeus Mozart, *Overture to Don Giovanni*
Czech Philharmonic Orchestra
https://www.youtube.com/watch?v=iW8wtvw52Pk

Tan Dun, *Opening Theme to Jet Li's Film, Hero*
Itzhak Perlman, Violin
https://www.youtube.com/watch?v=J9DDdNisv2U

Encore

Opera or Overture?

"Plenty of operas can boast of a single melody that has become more famous than the opera itself, the sort of tune people recognize as something from an opera, even if they have no idea which opera it is.

Then there are tunes that might be called 'operatic escapees,' melodies heard so often, and in so many places that they've earned a life of their own, independent of the operas for which they were created, to the point that they're barely associated with opera at all.

One example of such an escapee is the wistfully beautiful *Flower Duet* from Leo Delibes's opera *Lakme,* heard everywhere from movies to TV commercials to elevators. It's entirely possible that most who recognize the tune have never even heard of Delibes.

Then there's the *Dance of the Hours,* familiar to mil-

lions from the sublimely ridiculous hippo ballet in Disney's *Fantasia* and from Allan Sherman's pop hit, *Hello Mudda, Hello Fadda*. But how many among those millions know about its real home, in Amilcare Ponchielli's opera *La Gioconda?*"

The Tone Poem

I really can't blame the composers who wanted to do more than just write notes. They wanted to tell a good story with their music, wanted their music to tell the world about their feelings, impressions, and what they had on their mind at the time. They felt the symphony, with its rigid, defined structure, movements, and set formula, didn't cut it. Their answer? The tone poem.

From My Concert Seat

I don't know why I associate mismatched socks with one particular tone poem. Maybe it's because of the young man who sauntered over to the organ to play during that part of Ottorino Resphigi's *Pines of Rome* (1924) at a youth symphony orchestra concert I attended a few years ago. That particular young man was wearing a very noticeable pair of mismatched socks!

Recommended Listening

Alexander Borodin, *In the Steppes of Central Asia*
USSR Symphony Orchestra
https://www.youtube.com/watch?v=_W2aQf8Lb5M

William Grant Still, *Dismal Swamp (1937) Tone Poem for Piano and Orchestra*
Rachel Fields, piano
Cincinnati Philharmonic Orchestra
https://www.youtube.com/watch?v=20UM5XPLaUk

The Concerto

It was only a matter of time before a composer would pull one of the instruments out of the orchestra and write music for an artist to play it both with and apart from the orchestra, and when that happened, the concerto was born. The solo instrument could be any, even the mighty tuba! Ralph *(Raif)* Vaughn Williams (England, 1872-1958), wrote the *Tuba Concerto in F Minor* for that big instrument.

It does not surprise me at all that Beethoven and Brahms went one better and wrote concertos for three instruments simultaneously. Mozart and Mendelssohn doubled down, too, and wrote double-concertos for two pianos. The form they used, fast-slow-fast movements, was often the same, whether they wrote their concerto for one or more instruments; however, that is not set in stone. Some concertos start slow or at moderate speed and end slowly. They generally have three movements. This classical form is written solely for the virtuoso artist to show off his or her stuff, and I have had the extreme pleasure of hearing some of the best in live performance.

From My Concert Seat

I got a big kick out of watching famed pianist Andre Watts turning his head left and right and back and forth and making facial gestures at the orchestra while playing Beethoven's *Piano Concerto No.5 in E-flat Major, "The Emperor"* piano concerto with the Los Angeles Philharmonic. Jeremy Denk went in the opposite direction when he played Mozart's *Piano Concerto No.20* with that same Philharmonic in January of 2015 and appeared to rubberneck at the audience. The movements are surely not limited to the music, for the performers entertain with plenty of their own!

Recommended Listening

Edvard Grieg, *Piano Concerto A Minor*
Leif Ove Andsnes
St. Louis Symphony
https://www.youtube.com/watch?v=nokqNHsNEPw

Florence B. Price, *Piano Concerto in One Movement (1934), First Section*
New Black Music Repertory Ensemble
https://www.youtube.com/watch?v=189GH0gUBd4

The Opera

"Figaro, Figaro..." This one likely begs little explanation, for most know it is drama set to music, complete with showy costumes, dialogue, action, singing, and a storyline that audiences have seen and been thrilled by for centuries. In the midst of it all, an orchestra and plenty of divas belt out the tunes.

Recommended Listening

Giuseppe Verdi, *Otello "Act II: "Era la notte" (Iago)*
Placido Domingo, Leotyne Price
https://www.youtube.com/watch?v=qvakRCqoQEY

Kaija Saariaho, *Amour de Loin (Salonen)*
Scène du Pèlerin (Monica Groop), avec Clémence, Comtesse de Tripoli(Dawn Upshaw)
https://www.youtube.com/watch?v=JpkFJZDkqAI

Encore

Do We Really Need a Conductor?

The Orpheus Chamber, Prague Chamber, Amsterdam Sinfonietta, New Century Chamber, East Coast

Chamber, and the Advent Chamber Orchestras are well known and internationally acclaimed, but there is another shared commonality: They have no conductor. In fact, most seventeenth- and early eighteenth-century orchestras didn't have a conductor. The leader of the band was the concertmaster or the continuo player, generally the unnamed harpsichordist who led the orchestra with a few head nods and waves of the hand. That changed in the nineteenth century, when the conductor became a big name.

So, how did this individual become the prima donna, start making the big money, grabbing the glory and fame, and being wined and dined endlessly? Why is the conductor now seen as the single biggest asset of an orchestra? Well, from the technical, leadership and aesthetic perspective, the conductor's job is to set the right tempo (beat), the timing, tease out the musical nuances, emphasize key musical elements, and, in general, bring unity and coherence to the orchestra. He or she does that through their hand, facial, and body gestures, nuances, and by controlling the flow of the sound. Since there are dozens of musicians wailing away but only one conductor, somebody has to lead.

Science may provide a better answer though. In 2014, researchers at the University of Maryland conducted a study that used infrared lights to measure the musicians' reactions to the conductor. Their conclusion? "What we found is the more the influence of the conduc-

tor to the players, the more aesthetic, aesthetically pleasing the music was overall."

We can leave it to science, then, to confirm the value of at least one member of the modern orchestra. Certainly, the conductor wouldn't dispute his or her value, no matter how often it comes into question.

The Symphony

I really can't think of too many people who haven't at least heard of a symphony at some point. A symphony can be comprised of any number of movements—one, two, or three movements in modern times, though the old-school form usually involved four. A symphony can involve just a handful of instruments or an instrumental cast of hundreds. It can last for a few minutes or chug along for more than an hour. In the standard four-movement symphony, the first usually starts off at a fast trot; the second slows down, sometimes, way down; the third is a moderate to fast minuet (remember dancing away) or scherzo; and the fourth movement usually barrels home at an up-tempo pace. Meanwhile, some orchestras are really trying to get ahead of the tech curve and are big on mixed media with a symphony performance.

From My Concert Seat

I got a tiny glimpse of the future at a concert of the San Francisco Symphony Orchestra. The orchestra rolled the notes to Beethoven's *Symphony No. 5 in C Minor* (1804-

08) as they played it on a huge screen above the stage. The mixed media was an interesting touch. It will be even more interesting to see where orchestras will take this in the future.

Recommended Listening

Robert Schumann, *Symphony No.2 in C Major, Op 61*
Vienna Philharmonic
https://www.youtube.com/watch?v=L2eGkxHaGu0

Carlos Chávez, *Sinfonia No.2, "Sinfonía India" (1935-36)*
Orquesta Filarmonica de la ciudad de México
https://www.youtube.com/watch?v=TKoq4KOHUEU

Encore

Yes, Instruments Do Stand for Something

The instruments in a symphony do not just blare away; rather, they stand for something. That something is the composer's musical ideas, and the instruments give those ideas a voice and express them. Gustav Mahler was very explicit about that in his four-movement *Symphony No. 1, "The Titan."* To clarify, let's look at a snippet from the third movement. The principal idea behind it is a hunter's funeral, followed by a procession of animals. He presents it first with a solo double-bass. This is followed

by a bassoon and tuba. Then the full orchestra picks up the theme that is played over the top of the canon on the oboe. If you are aware of this, you can close your eyes, and open your imagination, you can almost see the animals parade by.

Now that I have briefly laid out my favorite classical forms and ensembles of the music that you hear in and out of classical music concert halls, it's time to start my guided tour of the classical music experience. As promised, I'll keep it as basic and as enjoyable as possible. After all, my goal is not just to share with you knowledge about classical music. I want you to walk away from this book appreciating the sheer joy and pleasure it has given me and other music listeners and lovers through several centuries. Our first point of reference on the tour will be the Baroque.

CHAPTER 1

A Guide to the Baroque

"Music is spiritual. The music business is not."
—Claudio Monteverdi

I didn't like Baroque music at all; it sounded tinny and screechy, as opposed to what musicians made onstage. I didn't even like the look of a few musicians making that sound. It took a long, long while for me to get over it, and the turnaround came quite by accident.

From My Concert Seat

The major concert season typically runs from September through May. That means three or more months without hearing a note of live classical music. By August one year, I was climbing the walls. I saw a notice for a chamber recital of works by Bach and Vivaldi. It was classical music, so I decided even that would be better than nothing. It was in an intimate setting at a library, and I was seated within an arm's reach of one of the violin players. I watched the joyful expression on her face as her

hands deftly glided the bow and effortlessly plucked the strings. It was captivating. However, what really grabbed me was the fulsome, flowing, energetic sound that poured out from the group. *God,* I thought, *is this what I've been sneering at with such great and undeserved scorn and disdain all these years?* On that fateful afternoon, I finally discovered the true power of the Baroque period.

First, let's go by the book. According to *Merriam-Webster,* the reigning authority in all meanings, there are three official definitions of *the Baroque* and the musical period and musical style it spawned. One is, "It's variously of, relating to, or having the characteristics of a style of artistic expression prevalent, especially in the seventeenth century that is marked generally by use of complex forms, bold ornamentation, and the juxtaposition of contrasting elements often conveying a sense of drama, movement, and tension." The second is, "It's characterized by grotesque, extravagance, complexity, or flamboyance. " My favorite of the three is the literal definition: "It's irregularly shaped—used of gems—a *baroque* pearl." The Baroque ran roughly from 1600 to 1750.

I quickly came to see that the Baroque period is the key to understanding what came after it in classical music. The terms you read now may be new to you if you are not a musician, critic, or musical aficionado, but I will speak plainly.

* * * * *

Baroque was first used by a French travel writer, Charles

de Brosses (1709-77). I don't know if he was a music lover or not, but he applied the term to architecture. Since Italy was then the center of musical action, it was only natural that it gets the credit for the term.

The major composers of this new, innovative sound were two early Italian operatic and madrigal composers, Jacopo Peri (1561-1633) and Claudio Monteverdi (1567-1643). They were both big on using new instruments and musical forms such as basso continuo (continuous bass), and recitative (talk, talk, and more talk). This is one of the distinguishing features of the early Baroque period.

From My Concert Seat

At a concert of the Baroque chamber ensemble, *Musica Angelica,* I spent way more time than I should have trying to figure out what the odd-looking period instrument one of the musicians was playing. That question went unanswered, but I finally decided it was better to just enjoy the sound of the instrument than worry about what it was called, and enjoy it I did.

Recommended Listening

Johann Pachelbel, *Canon in D Major*

It didn't stop there. As time passed, composers figured

out that the biggest instrument they had to work with was the sound that came from their throats. Thus, singing and singers became the new stars of the Baroque musical show. It was only a very short step to put it all together—singing, stagecraft, and instruments—and really turn opera into a big time production.

It is worth noting here that Baroque composers experienced the same ups and downs as anyone else. Therefore, they focused on using the new style to draw out the range of human emotions: joy, sorrow, anger, love, fear, affection, etc. There was a lot of variety to choose from: concert madrigals, one or more voices and occasionally instruments; and concertos, a sacred vocal work with instruments.

The composers suddenly had a lot more freedom and could really ramp up the sound. That was really important, as excellent vocals gave singers of the day a chance to show off their talents in a new and exciting way.

Recommended Listening

Archangelo Corelli, *12 Concerti Grossi*

There was no surprise that opera continued to be king of the musical hill in Italy, but the Italians weren't satisfied with being the champs of opera. They tinkered with it and went for more profound goals, like romantic and comic scenes and high and low characters to boost the entertainment value. The action unfolded in the simple recitative; again, it was a lot of talking. Then there was vocal chamber music. This took various forms, such as canzonettas, balletos, and villanelles—really just songs, but they were popular with the literate public. That public included everyone from kings and queens, nobles and ladies, to well-to-do merchants, traders, and crafters.

From My Concert Seat

I sometimes close my eyes at concerts and try to picture the high-brow crowd at Baroque-era concerts listening to the music while gabbing, socializing, and doing everything they could to be seen, impress, and flaunt their status. It had to be a sight to see.

In addition to Monteverdi, two other top Italian composers of the early Baroque were Francesco Cavalli (1602-76) and Antonio Cesti (1623-69). Handel came slightly later, and I'll have much to say about him soon. They tinkered some more and stressed lyrical arias and duets. Cesti's *Orontea* (1665) was the most popular opera of that period, and it included many arias that featured some humorous exchanges between the singers. The stage action was a musical give-and-take between singers, with an easy rhythm tailored to the vocalists. Meanwhile, Peri made greater use of the recitative style. In his *L'Euridice* (1600), he used the style of a speech-song, based on his readings of Greek theory on poetry.

I have only seen brief excerpts of their works on *You-*

Tube, and it was admittedly difficult to get a real feel for them in the context of our times rather than theirs. They seemed dated, turgid, and very slow. However, they were pioneering, and popular works of their day and are still being performed now, which speaks for itself.

Peri's style made the vocals sound like poetic recitations, as the talk was much more rhythmic and songful. I liken what he did in opera more than four centuries ago to today's rap and jazz scat singing, made famous by our beloved and unforgettable Ella Fitzgerald and Louis Armstrong.

This moved the opera from the domination of singers to the staging, costumes, and drama. Enter the French; they loved a show and were quick to see potential and the possibility of packing the opera house full. They usually introduced a production with a *sinfonia* (Italian for "symphony"), made ample use of the talking style, with arias, and drama. The point was to bring a lot of variety to the onstage action. Remember, the opera was, first and foremost, popular entertainment, and the producers always kept a sharp eye on the gate. This usually meant giving the audience some good singing and fast-paced action.

Monteverdi followed Peri with his *L'Orfeo* (1607). His operas moved easily from narrative to song, and since the listeners and onlookers of that time loved a good dance show as much as good singing, more opera duets and dance numbers were included. When they put the two together, the production was even more of a crowd-pleaser. It was always a big thrill to see two dueling singers face off, and it still is.

I'd be remiss if I didn't note that Monteverdi is still very much with us today, thanks, at least in part, to Sir John Eliot Gardiner. Since 1964, he has conducted the Monteverdi Choir and Orchestra, and over the years, they have performed Renaissance music before audiences on a global scale. Unfortunately, I've missed them the rare times they've played in southern California.

From My Concert Seat

While I have not personally witnessed the Monteverdi Choir and Orchestra performances, I did have the opportunity to hear their counterparts, The Tallis Scholars, who also perform music of that period. I heard them in the way such music should be heard: a Gothic setting at St. Basil's Catholic Church in midtown Los Angeles, in December of 2014. It did take some time for my ears to get used to the singsong style of the music of that day, but there wasn't an empty seat in the house that night. Obviously, Baroque vocalizing has its own sizable fandom, and I was not alone in enjoying it.

Recommended Listening

Claudio Monteverdi, *Banquet of the Senses (Madrigals)*

Opera took off and soon became all the rage in France.

One man who was determined to capitalize on its soaring popularity was Jean-Baptiste Lully (Italy-France,1632-87). He went light at first and combined comedy with ballets, but he, too, kept a keen eye on the gate. Lully found a lot of juicy material in mythology, tales of chivalry that he could bring to the stage. He began his operas with a grand, majestic overture, then tossed in a divertissement, a light ditty to give the audience a break from the heavy stuff onstage.

He continued to push the envelope in opera by reconciling drama, music, and ballet in what many now consider a new French form. The descriptive term was *tragedie lyrique* ("a lyric tragedy"). Don't think for a moment, though, that it was all doom and gloom on the stage, for there were still many interludes of dancing and choral singing *(divertissements)*. The operas were spacious, splashy, gaudy, attention-getting affairs; in other words, he put on a grand show.

There were, however, two crucial differences between Italian and French opera. One was the great emphasis on divertissements, all that dancing and choral singing. As for the other, Lully kept the focus on heroic themes that often included much praise of the king and the nobility. That only made sense, since he was on the king's payroll.

Encore

The Baton Makes a Tragic Introduction

Every concert-goer is familiar with the one piece of

equipment that is indispensable for a conductor, the baton. The conductor waves it around mostly to keep time, to give musicians their cues, and to amplify his or her bodily movements to the orchestra. However, the use of the baton actually started with a tragedy, one which befell Lully. In January of 1687, he was conducting a work to celebrate the king's recovery from an illness. He was busily banging his long staff on the floor to keep time with the orchestra. At one point, he banged his toe, and an abscess resulted from the blow. Whether it was through stubbornness, vanity, or ignorance, he refused to have it amputated; it did not help that penicillin was not available yet, so the end result was a nasty infection and a bad case of gangrene, a sure death sentence in those days. Lully passed away a short time later. Other conductors eventually got the message and sought a shorter stick that would not cause them bodily harm or mayhem, and the baton was born.

Now there was a surprise. As expected, most of the top composers at the time were men, but one woman actually managed to barge into the boys' club. That tenacious lady was Barbara Strozzi (Italy, 1619-77), a song-composing machine, with dozens of tunes under her dainty belt. Barbara wrote a lot about unrequited love, and those songs kept in step the feelings and emotions in the music of the period.

Of course the Church was never far out of the picture then; a lot of Lutheran and Catholic music was played within a small, sacred concert, with one or more soloists; these were known as cantatas. Sometimes, few instruments were used, and they were always set to some biblical theme. In the instrumental music of that period, usually keyboard compositions, there was the prelude, toccata, fugue, chorale, variations, and suite, all of which are instrumental forms.

Encore

A Woman's Place

Strozzi was well aware that she was bucking the tightly proscribed gender convention for women; women of that time did not dare to compose songs. In her first published work in 1644, she bluntly stated, "This is the first work that I, as a woman, all too daringly bring to the light of day." It also didn't surprise anyone that the gifted woman would be the target of snipping and malicious cracks about her sexuality.

A nobleman, Antonio Bosso, wisecracked that Strozzi had wonderful breasts; he never would have dreamt of making such a demeaning quip about any part of a male composer's anatomy. Then there was the anonymous wisecrack about her giving flowers to members of her father's academy: "It is a fine thing to have distributed the flowers after having already surrendered the fruit."

So far, I've focused on the beginnings of opera and a bit of chamber music and smaller works. It wasn't early opera alone, though, that made the Baroque what it was and set the later course of classical music. That credit goes to the big names that came out of that period. However, before we meet them, let's first meet some of the composers who also performed their works before the nobility of Europe in the eighteenth and nineteenth centuries. Just after the turn of the twentieth century, there was the coming of the Jazz Age in America, and they and their music drew the attention of more than a few classical music greats. These are the composers of African ancestry.

Florence Price

CHAPTER 2

A Guide to African-American Classical Composers

"In all types of Negro music, rhythm is of preeminent importance. In the dance, it is a compelling, onward-sweeping force that tolerates no interruption... All phases of truly Negro activity—whether work or play, singing or praying—are more than apt to take on a rhythmic quality."

—Florence Price

I'm sure I was not alone in once thinking that classical music is a pure, insular, elite European musical form. The even blunter accuse it of being stodgy, stuffy, upper-crust music written by a bunch of dead white guys. A look around any concert hall on any given concert night seemingly serves as proof of that. In most cases, one can spot only a handful of persons of color, especially African-Americans. I often saw Robert Lee Watt play with the L.A. Philharmonic Orchestra, a French hornist for more than thirty years with the orchestra. In his book, *The Black Horn: The Story of Classical French Hornist Robert Lee Watt,* he notes, "In all of my 3-plus decades in the orchestra, out of 3,800 patrons, maybe 20 black folks were present at any given concert. On several occasions, I met some of these uncomfortable black patrons at concert intermissions. They always approached me with great caution, and what annoyed me most about them was that they constantly whispered."

I look at this differently than Watt. The paucity of African-Americans and Hispanics at most classical concerts has absolutely nothing to do with the supposed pure-bred, racially exclusive Europeanism of the music that supposedly keeps concert halls looking like a white, elite country club. The true measure of classical music's universal, emotive, and cross-cultural adaptability is its own history. The list of Hispanic, Africans, African-Americans and Afro-European conductors, instrumental performers, and singers is and always has been, rich, varied, and deep. Sadly, the recognition of this has almost always come in relation to the work of a major composer. Two textbook examples of this are three major works by two of the classical giants. Two are by Camille Saint-Saens (France, 1835-1921), and the other is by Antonin Dvorak (Czechoslovakia, 1841-1904).

In the second movement of Dvorak's *Symphony No. 9, "From the New World"* (1893), there's the unmistakable melody of a Negro spiritual. Later, one of Dvorak's pupils, William Arms Fisher, penned the words to the song *"Goin' Home"* to it. This is what Fisher had to say about it: "…the lyric opening theme of the Largo (second movement) should spontaneously suggest the words 'Goin' home, goin' home' is natural enough, and that the lines that follow the melody should take the form of a Negro spiritual accords with the genesis of the symphony."

From My Concert Seat

I've heard Dvorak's *New World Symphony* in concert many times. Each time, I've thought about how that second movement came about. The really sad part about this is that even Fisher's frank admission of the influence of black music on what is considered Dvorak's greatest work might not have been enough to get critics to acknowledge it if Dvorak himself hadn't openly acknowledged that influence: "In the Negro melodies of America, I discover all that is needed for a great and noble school of music." He later waffled and tried to say there was nothing of the Negro in it, but he knew better.

Recommended Listening

Florence Price, *Symphony No. 3 in C. Minor*

Encore

More to the Dvorak and Black Music Story

Henry "Harry" Thacker Burleigh (1866 –1949) had a

beautiful baritone voice and phenomenal music talent. He did what few other blacks of the era could even hope to do when he was accepted to enroll at one of America's most prestigious musical institutes at the young age of twenty-six, the National Conservatory of Music in New York. He sang and played double-bass in the Conservatory orchestra. It was a struggle to make ends meet, so he worked for the school registrar as a handyman and janitor.

Burleigh's labor as a cleaner and musician didn't go unnoticed. He caught the eye Conservatory Director Dvorak, who was so impressed that he asked Burleigh to sing for him. Burleigh later noted, "I sang our Negro songs for him very often, and before he wrote his own themes, he filled himself with the spirit of the old spirituals." It is noted that in a candid moment, Dvorak acknowledged that spirit. It comes through not just in the New World Symphony but also at the beginning of each movement of his *American String Quartet*.

Meanwhile, Saint-Saens hit the road every chance he got; he was one of those guys who simply didn't feel right if he wasn't on a boat or a train going somewhere. One of his globe-trotting treks took him to Africa. As soon as he got a gander at the sights and lent an ear to the sounds, he was hooked. In 1891, he tried to capture a bit of the feel and the sense of being in what was then still seen as an exotic, even primal, faraway place in his single movement *Fantasia Africa*

(1891) for piano and orchestra. It's not a long piece, but it's especially memorable for his skillful blend of North African folk music. It has a rousing climax, with a Tunisian folk tune.

Five years later, Saint-Saens was back on the continent again. This time, he had in mind an even bigger, more expansive work that really packed in a lot of the folk music and sounds of North Africa. The result was his grand and popular *Piano Concerto No. 5 in F Major* (1896). It quickly got the tag *"The Egyptian,"* and there is no mistaking why. The second movement, starts off loud, with a big sound. This is quickly backed up by the piano, which taps out a theme based squarely on a Nubian love song. Saint-Saens heard the boatmen sing it during a cruise down the Nile. Near the end of the work, he pulls out the stops, with the piano and orchestra working overtime to create a colorful, free-flowing sound complete with frogs and crickets, which serenaded him in a chorus of chirps on the banks of the Nile.

I don't think I'll get much of an argument when I say jazz had a big impact on classical music. George Gershwin (America, 1898-1937), Aaron Copland (America, 1900-90), and Maurice Ravel acknowledged this and left no doubt that they owed a deep debt of gratitude to jazz. That debt has always been on magnificent display in Gershwin's two big piano works, *Rhapsody in Blue,* and *Concerto in F;* his orchestral work, *An American in Paris;* and his best-known musical gem, the opera, *Porgy and Bess.* There's Copland's *Concerto for Clarinet and Orchestra,* and Ravel's *Piano Concerto for the Left Hand* and *Piano Concerto in G.* Gershwin, Copland, and

Ravel were the best known among those who blended jazz with the classics, but they were hardly alone. *Wikipedia* lists twenty-eight major composers who have explicitly used jazz themes, rhythms, tempos, and even complete jazz forms in their compositions. These are:

Malcolm Arnold	1959	*Concerto No. 2 for Clarinet and Orchestra, Op. 115*
Leonard Bernstein	1948–49/1965	*Symphony No. 2, The Age of Anxiety*
Aaron Copland	1926 1946	*Concerto for Clarinet and Orchestra*
George Gershwin	1924	*Rhapsody in Blue*
	1925	*Concerto in F*
	1928	*An American in Paris*
	1931	*Second Rhapsody*
	1933-34	*Variations on "I Got Rhythm"*
	1935	*Porgy and Bess*
Paul Hindemith	1922	*Suite für Klavier*
Darius Milhaud	1922	*Trois Rag Caprices, Op. 78, for Piano*
Maurice Ravel	1929–31	*Piano Concerto for the Left Hand*
	1929–31	*Piano Concerto in G*
Dmitri Shostakovich	1934	*Suite for Jazz Orchestra*
Igor Stravinsky	1919	*Piano-Rag-Music*
Kurt Weill	1928	*The Threepenny Opera*

This is just the tip of the iceberg. Classical music artists of African descent began to compose and play not 20, 50, or even 100 years ago but 500 years ago. Black trumpeter John Blanke served England's Kings Henry VII and VIII as a court musician, and a tapestry captured an image of him performing in 1511.

Ignatius Sancho, born on a slave ship near West Africa, was raised in England and feted by the British aristocracy. He began composing in earnest in the 1770s. Fourteen of his pieces, including six minuets, have been recorded and were made available in 2007 by the Museum of Richmond as part of their "Trading in Human Lives: The Richmond Connection." His outstanding works can be heard at http://sancho-music.tripod.com.

Sancho made an even more lasting mark by doing what few classical music heavyweights ever did: He actually wrote a book on music composition, *A Theory of Music*. I was so impressed with this that I searched high and low through the archives to find it, to no avail. That search will likely continue.

As great and remarkable as these achievements were, classical music artists of African descent who have composed, conducted and performed are not even household names in a small neighborhood. Nonetheless, they have made undeniable, lasting, and profound contributions to classical music by broadening it, based on the varied types of material they used in their monumental works.

Encore

THE BRIDGETOWER SONATA?

George Bridgetower was a prodigious musical talent of Afro-Caribbean ancestry who gave successful violin concerts in Paris, London, Bath, and Bristol in 1789. He performed in around fifty concerts in London theaters between 1789 and 1799. In the spring of 1789, Bridgetower performed, to great acclaim, at the Abbaye de Panthemont in Paris, where Thomas Jefferson and his family were in attendance. The one composer, though, who would have burned Bridgetower's name in the classical music books for eternity was Beethoven—that is, if things hadn't gone badly awry.

On a visit to Vienna in 1803, Bridgetower performed with Beethoven. The master was impressed, so much so that he dedicated his *Violin Sonata No. 9 in A Major* to Bridgetower, a true honor. Though no offense was intended, he even plopped on the humorous title *Sonata per un Mulattico Lunatico.* Beethoven was so eager to display it that he gave a public performance at the Augarten Theater on May 24, 1803, the ink barely dry. Bridgetower played the violin part so well that Beethoven leapt up an exclaimed, "Noch einmal, mein lieber Bursch!" ("Once more, my dear fellow!"). The master wasn't finished; he was so grateful that he forked over his tuning fork to Bridgetower, an artifact that is on display today in the British Library.

Alas, the happy story didn't have a happy ending. Both B's were top-rate virtuoso performers, and both had strong temperaments and egos. They fell out over Bridgetower's purported insult of a female friend of Beethoven's. In a pique, what would have been known for posterity as the *Bridgetower Sonata* was instead renamed by Beethoven as *Kreutzer Sonata,* after Beethoven's other violin-playing pal, violin virtuoso Rudolphe Kreutzer. There's a final sad note: Kreutzer said the work was too difficult and never played it. Regardless, the sonata still bears his name today, instead of the man who could have expertly performed it.

Recommended Listening

L.V. Beethoven, *Violin Sonata No. 9, "Kreutzer"*

Even if it was only a brief moment in time, I'm happy to note that the curtain of invisibility of composers of African ancestry was slightly lifted a few decades back, with a brief recognition of the works of Samuel Coleridge Taylor (England, 1875-1912). A couple festivals in this country have been hosted in honor of his work, and there has been the occasional recording and performance of his best-known trilogy of cantatas, *Hiawatha's Wedding Feast* (1898-1900). Sadly, not much more than that has been played.

However, I loved it when Jeanne Lamon lifted the cloak

of invisibility back slightly further when her Tafelmusik Baroque Orchestra recorded *Le Mozart Noir* (2003), the music of the flamboyant, charismatic, and true Renaissance Afro-French composer, violinist, and conductor, Chevalier de Saint-Georges (France, 1745-99) He was a master swordsman and military colonel, and pulled off the deft feat of being both royalist and supporter of the French Revolution. de Saint-Georges was a prolific composer and penned operas, symphonies, concertos, and ballets. There is also a docudrama on his life. As earlier noted, he conducted the premiere of Haydn's *Symphony No. 82, "The Bear,"* in Paris in 1787.

From My Concert Seat

In April of 2009, I hosted an event at a coffee house in south Los Angeles, the African-American Classical Music Luncheon. There was a presentation on de Saint Georges, and I showed *Le Mozart Noir: Reviving a Legend,* produced in 2003 by BC Television of Canada. The docudrama was a real eye-opener for the participants, most of whom came from many of the local classical music orchestras and groups. I still take great pride in being able to do my little part to expose a few more to his music, as well as the works of other black composers.

Recommended Listening

Samuel Coleridge Taylor, *Scenes from The Song of Hiawatha*

Much closer to home, for decades, William Grant Still (America, 1895-1978) has been the one and sometimes the only recognizable name among African-American classical music composers. His *Afro-American Symphony* (1930) gets most of the air and concert play for classical work by a black composer and is almost always played on classical music stations during Black History Month in February. That's yet another shame, as there is so much more available that goes neglected and forgotten year after year. Suggested works by Still include: *Symphony in G minor* (1937); *Festive Overture* (1944); *Poem for Orchestra* (1944); and *Symphony No. 5, "Western Hemisphere"* and *A Southern Interlude,* opera (1942). If you seek these out and listen to them, you will hear just how much there is to admire about his work, just as I do.

Here, I would like to mention more notable works by African-American classical composers that span all forms, symphonies, concertos, cantatas, operas, and chamber works and are marked with rich harmonies, melodies, and stirring tempos: Ulysses Kay (American, 1917-95), the operas *Jubilee* and *Frederick Douglass;* George Walker (1922), *String Quartet No. 1* and *Address for Orchestra;* Florence Price (America, 1887-1953), *Concerto in F* and *Symphony No. 1;* Margaret Allison Bonds (America, 1913-72), *The Negro Speaks of Rivers,* voice and piano (published in 1942) and *The Ballad of the Brown King,* chorus, soloists, and orchestra (1954).

There is, of course, great cause to include Edward Kennedy "Duke" Ellington (American,1899-1974). He has come almost full circle in recent years, from his lofty place as an American jazz icon to a recognizable American classical music icon. Take a listen to *Harlem: Suite from the River* and *Black, Brown, and Beige Suite* (1943); these are part of his *Four Symphonic Works* as a representative sampling of the Duke's perfect blend of jazz and the classics.

It didn't stop with the "Duke." Thomas Jefferson (T.J.) Anderson has been in the composing business dating back to Ellington's day. He's written over eighty works ranging from operas and symphonies to choral pieces, chamber music, and band music. One of his highly acclaimed special commissioned work is *In Front of My Eyes: An Obama Celebration,* soprano, flute, piccolo and alto flute (2010). Anderson has been outspoken in challenging the classical world to lift the cloak of invisibility that shrouds African-American classical composers. He hasn't been alone in making the plea with their voice and their music. The new wave of black composers Jonathan Bailey Holland with his mixed media, eclectic undulating tone poem *Shards of Serenity* (2013) have drawn raves the times it has been performed. Composer and musical scholar George Lewis has also raised more than a few eyebrows with his *"Memex" for orchestra* (2014) that almost literally pummels the ear with sounds and instruments that blast notes from every conceivable direction

I highly recommend *AfriClassical Blog,* a companion to the website AfriClassical.com, as it offers interesting biographical snapshots of many black composers. A companion to this is *Black Opera and Concert Singers: A Resource Book,* a rich compilation and history of more than 700 operas by black composers.

There are encouraging signs that the contributions of black composers to classical music are gaining more widespread recognition. Works by black composers are being included on the concert bills by major orchestras and chorales. There's also the growth in the number of African-American classical music orchestras and ensembles that perform concerts featuring the works of black composers. This is good news, an assurance that the black experience in classical music will continue to enrich the lives of African-Americans and of all music lovers for as long as there is music.

Now let's return to the Baroque. Bach and Handel are two names that many have heard of, whether you are wild about classical music or couldn't care less about it. I'll spend the requisite time on both men, but others were just as influential in their own way. In fact, Bach and Handel wouldn't be the Bach and Handel they were if not for some of these other names in classical music.

Johann Sebastian Bach

CHAPTER 3

A Guide to More Baroque

"If you don't like this, I'll stop writing music."
—Antonio Vivaldi

As I said, my guess is that no matter whether you love, hate, or simply couldn't care less about classical music, you've still almost certainly heard two of the greatest names in the art: Germans Johann Sebastian Bach (1685-1750) and George Frederick Handel (1685-1759). However, for just a second, forget these familiar names and classical music altogether. Bach in particular has become a bit of a franchise all his own, a big money-growth industry over the years. He turns up in movies, commercials, dance halls, churches, TV series, game shows, and more etc. Bach is the one name a classical music lover thinks of when the Baroque is mentioned. Nevertheless, Bach is not really the fair and equitable starting point to efficiently and fairly assess the Baroque giants and their contributions and influence. This distinction belongs to Antonio Vivaldi (Italy, 1678-1741), a fiery redhead, well-traveled, nearly a priest, and longtime teacher at a mostly girls orphanage, the Ospedale Della Pietà (Devout Hospital of Mercy) in Venice.

Vivaldi was another virtual composing machine, the author of at least 500 concertos, 21 operas, and 90 sonatas, as well as many choral works. He was fast with the pen and supposedly boasted that he could write a concerto even faster than its parts could be copied. Whether he actually said that or not, the fact remains that he was super quick on the draw when it came to composing—so quick, in fact, that a cruel knock suggests he wrote the same piece 500 times. Russian great Igor Stravinsky was even more specific and cruel. He purportedly quipped that he wrote the same concerto over and over, 400 of them repeatedly. On the contrary, Vivaldi's pieces are anything but reruns of each other, and I love them. They are breezy and energetic and possess great range, depth and variety in the sound. Some of them you can dance away to; I know because I have.

Recommended Listening

Antonio Vivaldi, *The Four Seasons*

Bach knew a good thing when he heard it. He studied Vivaldi night and day, copied his scores, and borrowed heartily from them in his works. Vivaldi's smash hit, *The Four Seasons* (1720), is an eternal staple on concert stages and has been used in movies, commercials, and TV shows.

There's much more to Vivaldi than that, though, and frankly, some of the "that" is simply more intensely inventive and enjoyable listening to his music.

From My Concert Seat

One of the pieces that always gives me sheer delight and puts me in a peaceful, joyful mood is Vivaldi's *Lute Concerto in D Major* (1730s). It's also played on guitar and mandolin. Vivaldi must have been mellowed out when he penned the second movement of the piece, for a work couldn't be more serene. It is a perfect showpiece for the sublime power of a Baroque instrumental piece.

I certainly appreciate Vivaldi, and I recognize his bracing impact on the Baroque and classical music in the periods after the Baroque. However, the name of the game in the Baroque sound is still Bach, seconded only by Handel. In Donald J. Grout, et.al's, *A History of Western Music,* basically one of the Bibles among college classical music texts, a summary says, "For many listeners today, Bach and Handel are the Baroque." Of course volumes have been written on Bach and Handel and their gargantuan influence on Western music—not just classical but also pop, rock and roll, country, opera, and more. In fact, when Johannes Brahms was asked about Western music and composing, he had one simple answer that says it all: "Study Bach. There you will find everything." Likewise, Beethoven said of Handel, "He is the greatest composer that ever lived. I would uncover my head and kneel before his tomb." Mozart also offered accolades: "Handel understands effect better than any of us... When he chooses, he strikes like a thunderbolt."

When heavyweights like these pay such a lofty tribute that pretty much settles it: Bach and Handel were the big men on campus in classical music, particularly in the Baroque. Nevertheless, here's the rub: Neither Bach nor Handel created a totally original musical form. Handel's operas and oratorios and Bach's cantatas, masses, oratorios, keyboard, and violin concertos were cobbled together from Italian, French, German, and other musical forms. They include the old stuff, like madrigals, Italian and French operas, orchestral suites, and keyboard music, but what they borrowed or pilfered from these sources, they did a lot differently, a whole lot better, and with a whole lot nobler eloquence.

We'll start with Handel's oratorio, but don't worry: I'll get to his famous *Messiah* shortly. The oratorio, strictly defined, is an opera without stage drama and costumes. It's a sacred subject presented in concert in a church or religious setting and generally not onstage. By contrast and as noted earlier, the opera is a popular musical work for the dramatic stage that combines text, plot, the spoken word, singing, acting, costumes, dance, and an accompanying orchestra or musical ensemble—some real fun stuff.

Handel borrowed lavishly from French classical drama, ancient Greek tragedy, the German Passion play, the English dance and olden religious songs for his oratorios. His important innovation was the use of the chorus. He also knew that the crowd would be most attentive during the religious season of Lent, so he leased a London theater for their presentation, scheduling things for that time of the year. His oratorios, though, were not church music. Rather, they were earmarked for the concert hall, and they had a lot of popular appeal. Handel was a savvy businessman, smart enough to recognize that there was an audience outside the powdered, pompadour, wig-wearing, moneyed crowd. That audience consisted of the slightly well-to-do commoners who also had some money to burn and leisure time to occupy.

Recommended Listening

G.F. Handel, *The Arrival of the Queen of Sheba, 3 from the Oratorio, Solomon*

Messiah is, of course, Handel's most important oratorio. Everyone in Christendom knows of it, and it is a fixture on nearly every church and concert bill during the Christmas season and often during Easter; in fact, that was the season when Handel premiered it in Dublin, Ireland, in April of 1742. Handel knew what any brilliant businessperson knows today: Timing is everything. It was billed then with an oxymoron if there ever was one: "sacred entertainment."

Encore

Why Do We Stand for the Hallelujah Chorus of *Messiah*?

The stock answer as to why audiences automatically jump to their feet during the Hallelujah chorus of Handel's *Messiah* is that King George II was so moved during the London premiere in March of 1743 that he spontaneously jumped to his feet when he heard it. In an era of absolute monarchies, when the king jumped, so did everyone else. Thus was a tradition firmly established, one that has carried into present day.

Of course, this could be yet another urban legend, just another of the many delightful but false yarns that abound in the history of classical music. There is really no solid proof that ol' George was even there; obviously, there were no paparazzi in his day. No account, eyewitness or in print, corroborates his attendance. It took almost forty years for a writer to mention it, a story that came to that writer secondhand. I'd like to think people leapt to their feet at the premiere anyway, kingly presence notwithstanding, for such a pulsating, rollicking homage to God will move any religious soul, and most folks back then were deeply religious. It's also worth noting that audiences stood for others of Handel's moving, religious, singsong pieces, such as the *"Dead March"* in his 1739 oratorio *Saul*. For my part, though, why mess up

a good yarn about the ol' king with the truth? A good yarn is always worth sharing and sometimes worth believing.

Handel hit the road early on and headed for Italy, for he had to pay the obligatory homage to the old opera masters and their style. He also knew a good thing when he saw it; he studied Vivaldi and stole from him with reckless abandon. The composer he borrowed even more from was actually Handel; in other words, he recycled much of his own work. A good example of this is probably his single most recognizable piece, the *"Hallelujah"* chorus from *Messiah.* Handel lifted the line in it, "Lord God King of Hosts," a praise from an earlier opera of his, a ribald homage not to God but to debauchery. This was in the pre-copyright, pre-litigious era, so when Handel or Bach or any other composer borrowed from another, they were still home free. They didn't have to worry about messy lawsuits, gargantuan payouts, or the threat of being slapped with a cease-and-desist order.

In time, Handel settled in England and straddled two worlds with his music. One was the world of aristocracy and nobility. The dukes, earls, a queen, and especially Kings George I and II absolutely adored him. That was the one world a composer had to infiltrate to have any hope of getting their works written and widely performed. After all, the money of the rich still paid the bills.

Handel pretty much stuck to the religious script with his operas *Rinaldo* (1711), *Julius Caesar* (1724), *Saul* (1738), *Israel in Egypt* (1739), and *Judas Maccabaeus* (1746), all based on familiar biblical themes and something larger audiences could readily identify with. They featured arias, drama, instrumental music, and much talk. Handel really scored big, though, with his *Water Music Suites* (1717). It is thought that it was written for the entertainment of the king and the court for their pleasant boat ride down the Thames River in London.

It didn't much matter whether he penned it specifically for a kingly river jaunt or not, since he had an even bigger hit with *Royal Fireworks* (1749); initially, it was literally performed with fireworks, further ensuring that it would be unforgettable. So many thousands turned out for the rehearsals that it caused a massive traffic jam on the London Bridge, and with no traffic lights or cops to control the throngs, it made for a big street party.

The consummate entrepreneur, he also knew how to spread things around. He wrote sonatas, *Concerti Grossi* (concert instrumental numbers) and keyboard music. He used some of these as fillers or possibly even time-killers to entertain the audience between acts in his fulsome choral and stage works.

Encore

A Handel and Jimi Hendrix Jam Session

The thought of a Jimi Hendrix and Handel jam session sounds absolutely ridiculous, right? Not so fast! Many Londoners and music aficionados have long known that, for two years, from 1968 until his death in 1970, Jimi

Hendrix lived in a flat on Brook Street in London, right next to the flat Handel lived in two centuries earlier. Today, the two flats are joined, known as the Handel House Museum, which draws thousands of visitors every year. For a time, it was assumed that a big-name rocker like Hendrix didn't know or care to know about a guy who composed music a time and a world apart from his own, but we now know better. Hendrix snatched up a bunch of Handel recordings, including *Messiah,* but that wasn't all. A few listeners claim they can hear a riff or two from Handel in some of the guitar work of the later Hendrix recordings. This might be a stretch, but being a longtime Hendrix music junkie myself, I'll take that stretch.

Just for fun listen to the contemporary classical music specialty ensemble, The Kronos Quartet, play Hendrix's signature works, *Purple Haze* and *Foxy Lady live* in concert.

Recommended Listening

J. Hendrix, *Foxy Lady*
Kronos Quartet
https://www.youtube.com/watch?v=QcAxJ1_8NBc

J.Hendrix, *Purple Haze*
Kronos Quartet
https://www.youtube.com/watch?v=eMyBoHw0rsQ

I'll briefly discuss three other musician-composers who were also important to the Baroque story, before we tread over to the well-known Bach. The first is Domenico Scarlatti (1685-1757). Though born in Italy, he lived first in Portugal, then spent the last years of his life in Spain. His major contribution was harpsichord sonatas. He was another composing machine, and at least 555 of his sonatas have survived the ebb of time.

Recommended Listening

Domenico Scarlatti, *Sonata in D Minor K. 9, Allegretto*

Scarlatti's true passion was to include lots of harmonies and much diversity in his sound. This comes as no surprise, since he was deeply influenced by Spanish music, which is featured in many of his sonatas. Harmony was his strong suit, and it adds more flavor and color to these works.

Meanwhile, back in Germany, Dieterich Buxtehude's (Germany-Denmark, 1637-1709) was making his mark with his organ toccatas. These present the music in short sections, in a free style that alternates with longer sections. Toccatas stress motion, improv, lots of irregular, fast rhythm, and a stupendous climax. Bach was a big fan of his and liked what he heard in his work, so the style also shows up in some of Bach's pieces. In fact, Bach was such a fan that he once walked 200-plus miles to hear Buxtehude perform. In truth, Scarlatti's and Buxtehude's greatest value is what they brought to

Bach's music table, the influence they had on one of the greatest of the greats.

From My Concert Seat

I was amazed to learn of Bach's long walk. I was even more amazed to read that in March of 2005, a group of Hilde Binford's music history students at Moravian College in Bethlehem, Pennsylvania came up with the bright idea of imitating his famed trek. Almost to the day Bach had done it 300 years earlier, they set out. It took them three days, hoofing part of it and using train and ferry to supplement the remainder of their journey, to get to a New York Philharmonic concert. Surely the old man had to be smiling down on them from somewhere.

The other musician-composer that put his stamp on the music of the time was Francois Couperin (France, 1668-1733), whose keyboard music combined the French and Italian styles. His twelve suites for harpsichord include a prelude and dance movements. He fits into the picture here for the one other important distinction he brought to the table. Some of his piano pieces have very explicit and picturesque titles, such as "*The Mysterious Barricades.*" He uses harmonies to express an emotional mood, be it melancholy, introspective, or searing passion. This was a forerunner of what would later come to be known as the tone poem, and we will discuss this phenomenal link later.

Now, we finally come to the man all the old masters and the new ones since have bowed down to as the grand master of the old classical music genre. This, of course, is Bach. Remarkably, as well-known as he is, he didn't venture a step out of Germany during his lifetime. He was regarded as one of the greatest organists of his day. Be careful not to get too carried away though; some refer to him as "the greatest of all time," but a great musician, like music, is also in the ear of the beholder. He certainly composed a rich, varied amount of music for the Church. Both *St. Matthew Passion* (1727) and *St. John Passion* (1724) are regulars in the performance repertoire today, especially during religious seasons. I've had the pleasure of hearing these in church settings and concert halls from groups, as varied as church musical ensembles to the Los Angeles Master Chorale, and I have heard them a lot.

Vivaldi, as I mentioned, had a deep influence on Bach, especially when it came to his preludes and fugues for organ, his keyboard concertos, and his two big chorales (some of which he lifted directly from Vivaldi, as previously noted). Bach's *Well-Tempered Clavier* (1722), his English and French suites, show the influence of French and Italian models. His *Goldberg Variations* (1741) are a joy to hear, with the variety of notes and the sound they produce; when my daughter heard them, she was instantly hooked, and piano players at all levels swear by them. Bach displayed the full range of genres, styles, and forms of the day in his music. His music has always been considered by the experts as the closest thing to a complete package in encompassing harmony, counterpoint, melody, rhythm, and inventiveness, and this opinion is held with good reason.

Recommended Listening

J.S. Bach, *Brandenberg Concerto No. 2*

Encore

Go Get the Other Guy

Here's a fun what-if. Twice, the young Bach applied for musical positions, one as organist in Muhlhausen in 1707 and the other in Leipzig. He was reluctantly hired as organist in Muhlhausen only after the position was vacant for six months. In Leipzig, it was even worse: He was not the first or even second choice of the Church Council at St. Thomas's Church for the post in 1723. Two others, including the renowned Georg Philipp Telemann (Germany, 1681-1767), had turned it down, so Bach was pretty much what was left. Still, even that wasn't the end of Bach's indignation. The church fathers grumbled publicly about having to hire "the mediocre one." What if they had gotten the other guy instead of Bach? Would the course of Western music have been altered? Happily, we'll never know.

For many, Bach's three sets of six harpsichord works are the be-all-that-end-all for the keyboard. These include *The English Suites* (1718-20), *The French Suites* (1722-25), and the Partitas. There is also his grand work, *The Well-Tempered Clavier* (1722). The Suite sets were showcased to demonstrate his great skill on the harpsichord. He may or may not have been the greatest on that instrument or the organ, but he was pretty darn good.

Bach's best-known works for the harpsichord include:

- *The Well-Tempered Clavier*
- *The Goldberg Variations*
- *The English Suites*
- *The French Suites*
- *The Brandenberg Concertos No.1 No.2. No.3. No.4. No.5, and No.6*

There's no end to Bach's musical generosity. He gave the music world not one, two, three but four other musical gifts, to varying degrees. A quartet of his twenty children followed in the old man's footsteps. It's oft said in classical music lore that if one mentioned the name Bach at the turn of the eighteenth century, the name that came to the music lover's mind was not the old man's; rather, they thought of his son, Carl Philipp Emanuel Bach. (Germany, 1714-88). He was, far and away, the most renowned Bach of the time—so popular that then and today, he does not have to be referred to by his full name to be recognized. He is known simply as C.P.E. Bach, rather than by his whole name, which is definitely a mouthful.

To be sure, C.P.E. was influential, with his strikingly expressive and impassioned, urgent sound. However, the Bach son who ranked right up there with him in having a big impact on the music scene was the youngest one, Johann Christian Bach (Germany, 1735-82). This was, in part, because of his musical talents and innovations, which were indeed considerable. He spread his talent around generously, writing concertos, symphonies, chamber music, keyboard music, and operas. He also befriended a man who was so inspired by and impressed with his style that he did a bit of copying; that man was Mozart. The remarkable result was that Mozart arranged three of Bach's sonatas as his three piano concertos: *Piano Concertos No. E, No. D,* and *No. G.* Just for fun, listen to one of those concertos and a Bach sonata, say *Sonatas No. 3* and *No. 6,* to get the drift of how one composer's music and style—light and airy in Bach's case—can influence another's, even Mozart's.

Recommended Listening

C.P.E. Bach, *Flute Concerto in D minor*

Bach's other two musical progeny, in addition to C.P.E and Johann Christian, were Wilhelm Friedemann Bach (Germany, 1710-84) and Johann Christoph Friedrich Bach (Germany, 1732-95). There were four of them, and they didn't miss a beat in trying to write all over the map. They wrote cantatas, chamber music, keyboard and orchestral works, operas and symphonies, keyboard sonatas, symphonies, oratorios, liturgical choir pieces and motets, operas and songs.

From My Concert Seat

I haven't heard much of the Bach brothers' works played in concert. I have to say, though, that while I hear much innovation and zest in their music, not much of it sounds terribly original in comparison to what the old man wrote. Still, I love the sound of Johann Christoph Bach's flute concertos, in part because I love the flute sound and in part because he's a Bach. Since he and his brothers carry the Bach surname, history is obligated to give them their musical due, and I figure I can do the same. I mentioned earlier that Mozart and Beethoven gushed over Bach and Handel, but this was with good reason beyond the obvious. Both of them stood on their shoulders when they took the extra step with their music to make and shape classical music as most know it today. In the pages that follow, we will explore the what, why, and how those big extra steps forward were accomplished.

However, first I'll take my second detour, in order to discuss another group of composers. These have not been as marginalized or ignored as most black composers in the classical music world, and many classical music greats have snatched at the style, color, and rhythm in their works and incorporated that into their sound. They have even paid tribute to them in the titles of their works such as *Symphonie Espanol* and *Capricio Espanol.* Still, these composers have also had to wage their fight for recognition. Our detour now will open our eyes to these wonderful Hispanic composers.

Silvertre Revueltas

CHAPTER 4

A Guide to Hispanic Classical Composers

"Many times during my childhood, I heard in the country Indian ensembles deeply rooted in the old traditions something that is now lost, which made it possible for me to delve in the aesthetics of those cultures: sobriety, conciseness, purity, and vigor."

—Carlos Chavez

I think it's accurate to say that composers in the Hispanic world fared far better in getting both name and musical recognition than composers of African descent. There are two reasons for this: First, Spain is European; second, Spanish influence has been magnetic for French and Russian composers, as evidenced by Edward Lalo's (1823-92) *Symphonie Espagnole* (1874); Ravel's *Rapsodie Espagnole* (1907-08); *Debussy's Iberia* (1905-08); and Rimsky-Korsakov's *Capricio Espanol* (1887).

The influence of Spanish culture, layered with Arab, Jewish, and Gypsy music has become readily recognizable in a number of classical compositions. There's also the cross-pollination between classical and native traditional musical forms such as Mexican waltzes, which follow the Viennese model but reflect a strong Spanish melodic influence and incorporate instruments used in Mexican folk music. This tradition is not new and can be heard in the motets, guitar, and lute pieces of seventeenth-century Spanish composers Lucas Ruiz de Ribayaz, Juan Gutierrez de Padilla, and Santiago de Murcia.

From My Concert Seat

I don't hear the works of the leading Spanish masters played very often in concert. That said, one conductor who has made it a point to spotlight some of them is Gustavo Dudamel, with the L.A. Philharmonic and his Simon Bolivar Orchestra. It is very gratifying on the occasions when my ears are blessed by the works of Enrique Granados, Albeniz, Federico Moreno Torroba, and Joaquin Rodrigo, which are frequently played in concert halls. The reach and influence of their music has extended to Latin America. Among the major Hispanic composers are Mexico's Carlos Chavez, Silvestre Reveueltas, Juan Pablo Moncayo, Ricardo Castro, and Blas Galindo; Argentina's Alberto Ginastera; and Cuba's Leo Brouwer. I fully expect to hear more of their works on concert bills in the future.

The following is a sample listing of the major works of

Spanish, Mexican, Cuban, and Argentine classical composers, who composed in every musical form there is: symphonies, concertos, quartets, songs, tone poems, and waltzes.

Isaac Albeniz	*Rapsodia Espanola (Spanish Rhapsody)*
Leo Brouwer	*Suite No. 2*
Gustavo Campa	*Melodia (Melody)*
Francisco Cardenas	*Viva mi Disgracia (Long Live My Disgrace)*
Ricardo Castro	*Vals Capricho (Waltz Caprice)*
Alfredo Caturia	*Tres Danzas Cubanas (Three Cuban Dances)*
Carlos Chavez	*El Tropico, from Caballos de Vapor (Horsepower)*
	Sinfonia India (Indian Symphony)
Ernesto Cordero	*Sonatina Tropical (Tropical Sonata)*
Santiago de Murcia	*Jacaras de la Costa (Dances of the Coast)*
Juan Gutierrez de Padilla	*A la Xacara, Xacarilla (Dance the Dance, Little Dancer)*
Lucas Ruiz de Ribayaz	*Chaconas y Marionas (Chaconnes and Dances)*
Carlos Espinoza	*Noche Azul (Blue Night)*
Blas Galindo	*Sones de Mariachi (Mariachi Songs)*
Enrique Granados	*Allegro de Concierto (Concert Allegro)*
Alberto Ginastera	*Bailes de Estancia (Dances from Estancia)*
Ernesto Lecuona	*Malaguena*
	Siboney
	Canto de Guajiro (Peasant's Song)
Jose de Jesús Martinez	*Magdalena*
Juan Pablo Moncayo	*Huapango*
Jorge Olaya Munoz	*Semblanzas (Aspects)*

Astor Piazzolla	*Otono Porteno (Buenos Aires Autumn)*
	Invierno Porteno (Buenos Aires Winter)
Manuel Ponce	*Concierto del sur (Southern Concerto)*
Juventino Rosas	*Sobre las Olas (On the Waves)*
Federico Moreno Torroba	*Suite Castellana (Castillian Suite)*

Encore

MAKING CLASSICAL MUSIC MEXICAN

Mexico's Silvestre Revueltas was certainly no member of the European club. From Paris in the 1930s, he wrote his wife Ángela:

"Now I realize how much my music is bound to disagree with all norms established by these civilizations. I'd love to perform it here, simply to see the expressions of disgust in their faces. It would be as if something obscene or tasteless or vulgar had been uttered."

Here's how one critic interpreted his observation/complaint:

"This 'vulgarity' in Revueltas's music, the bright and often brusque timbres that immediately strike us, cannot be understood without listening to the small village bands and *mariachis* that are so abundant in Mexico. Revueltas listened to them without prejudice and synthesized a daring and original concept of orchestration from their sounds. The importance of trumpets, tuba, and clarinets in his music, for instance, is drawn directly from

the instrumentation of such bands, as is his delight in the use of biting and purposefully unrefined articulation. Revueltas also exploits the out-of-tuneness of the village bands: by consistently choosing instruments of extreme register like the piccolo, the bass and E-flat clarinets, the tuba and the contrabass, shrillness, and spontaneous dissonance become a characteristic of color rather than intonation. And rather than ignoring or 'correcting' such provincial habits as lack of precise coordination or limping phrasing, he recognized their potential and found ways to positively integrate these spontaneous asymmetries into his musical language."

This says a mouthful, but he's on point in getting inside Revueltas's mind and music.

I want to get even more specific and spotlight five composers from four varied Latin countries: Brazil, Cuba, Spain, and Argentina. All of these have made important and noteworthy contributions to classical music. I include the major Mexican composers in my next chapter:

Leo Brouwer (Cuba, b. 1939) is responsible for a growing body of music that expands the technical reach of the guitar, such as extreme ranges and dynamics, as well as creating percussive effects on the guitar with both hands. His music blends Afro-Cuban and folk ingredients, and his styles ranged from avant-garde abstract works of the sixties to neoromanticism.

Alberto Ginastera's (Argentina, 1916-83) music spans the wide-ranging styles from songs, ballets *Panambi, Estancia,* operas, *Don Rodrigo* (1964), and a string *Quartet No. 2* of 1958. His works borrow heavily from native and folk traditions in music, song, and dance. His second opera, *Bomarzo* (1966-67), for the Opera Society of Washington, "met with ebullient praise, but its explicit eroticism provoked heated controversy," wrote *The New Grove Dictionary of Music and Musicians.*

Agustin Lara's (Cuba, 1897-1970) strong suit was song. He wrote an estimated 700 songs, 420 of them still known. He merged the Habanera, tango, foxtrot and the Cuban bolero.

HectorVilla-Lobos (Brazil, 1887-1959) wrote more than 1,000 works of all types, but is most celebrated for his *Bachianas Brasileiras,* nine pieces in homage to J.S. Bach. He created captivating music by synthesizing Brazilian folk melodies and dance rhythms with traditional art forms.

Julian Orbon (Spain-Cuba, 1925-91) From 1946 to 1960, he directed the Orbon Conservatory in Havana. Orbon took a step way backward in the evolution of classical music to incorporate in his compositions elements of a Medieval era chant.

Far and away, the greatest sea change in classical music south of the U.S. border and an ocean away from Europe came from Mexico. Yes, the now legendary twentieth-century Mexican composers were influenced by the old masters, but they brought a style of their own that blended the traditional with folk, Indian, and even political protest. That's quite a mix. I'll give a thumbnail sketch of the big three.

Manuel Ponce (1882-1948) was Mexico's first nationalistic composer. He wove popular Mexican themes throughout his styles, from his early romantic music in a later, more contemporary style. He is best known internationally for his song *Estrellita,* although he composed a variety of music, including music for the piano and a large repertory for the guitar. Spanish guitar virtuoso Andres Segovia credits Ponce with reviving the guitar as a solo concerto instrument, particularly in his *Concierto del Sur* (1941).

Silvestre Revueltas (1899-1940) was an outspoken, left-wing radical. He actually fought on the Republican side in the Spanish Civil War in the late 1930s. He wrote ten film scores. His *Sensemaya* skillfully wove popular Mexican folk music like street tunes and mariachi styles together. He used the same model for some of his other scores. He didn't exactly ape the nouveau sound of Igor Stravinsky, but he did lean heavily on his rhythm and instrumental style for a time. His music always has a heart-eating, innovative sound to it.

From My Concert Seat

One of my favorite composers is Carlos Chavez (1899-1978). I have played his *Symphonia No.2, "Sinfonia India"* (1935-36) often as fill music on my radio show. The color, vibrancy, and even swinging sounds of Indian music explodes with this piece. Chavez, more than the others

I mentioned, is the uncrowned, most influential south-of-the-border Mexican composer who chronicled the cultural life of Mexico in his music in the mid-twentieth century. He expanded the ethnic boundaries of classical music by introducing and championing Aztec music and native folk instruments in two Aztec ballets and everywhere else he could in his compositions.

While Chavez and Reveueltas are musical deities in Mexican classical circles, their music and style was really only a launch pad for an even younger generation of classical music artists in Mexico. There were at least five full-time, professional orchestras, such as the *La Orquesta Filarmonica de la UNAM,* in the greater Mexico City area alone in 2010, as well as many smaller ensembles in other cities and parts of the country. It was a thrilling moment for me to hear some of the music of contemporary composers at the *Palacio Nacional* at a concert in Mexico City several years ago. It was the perfect musical storm of Indian, folk, and old-style classical sound.

Famed Mexican conductor Enrique Batiz has been on a virtual one-man crusade to tout the new wave of Mexican classical composers and their unique sounds. I have heard many of them in his colossal set of eight CDs, *Musica Mexicana.* They include a broad range of sounds and styles, such as Roldofo Halffter's *Violin Concerto* (1939) to the rocking mambo and dance rhythms in Eugenio Toussaint's *Mambo Suite,* played by the ensemble *Sinfonietta Ventus* in the *Musica para Divertirse.*

L.A. Philharmonic Conductor Gustavo Dudmael has been on a sort of mini-crusade to champion and play the *Danzones* of Arturo Marquez, especially his wildly popular *Danzon No. 2; Danza del Mediodia* for woodwind quintet (Urtext); and *Espejos en la Arena,* for cello and orchestra. I've heard *Danzon No. 2* in concert, and "Wow!" is the only word to describe it. If you close your eyes, you can see two lovers swaying away to the smooth, elegant rhythm. Still, the piece that has taken the classical stage and airwaves by storm is José Pablo Moncayo's (Mexico, 1912-58) *Huapango* (1950). The first time I heard it, I knew I had to have it in my collection, for the piece is as close to a complete package blend of Mexican and classical sound as one can find. It rocks with Indian dances, songs, rhythms, folk, and classical, all set to a big orchestral sound.

Encore

What Would Mozart Have Said About These Instruments?

In *Sinfonia India,* Chavez pulled out all the stops in introducing and using native Indian instruments: the *jicara de agua,* half a gourd, inverted and partly submerged in a basin of water, struck with sticks; *güiro; cascabeles,* a pellet rattle; *tenabari,* a string of butterfly cocoons; a pair of *teponaxtles, tlapanhuéhuetl;* and *grijutian,* a string of deer hooves. Chavez understandably figured it might be tough to convince the percussionists in the orchestras of

the 1930s to wail away on these instruments, so when the score was published, he substituted their nearest equivalents in commonly used orchestral percussion. However, that didn't mean he wanted them dropped completely, and he insisted that the originals be used wherever possible. They have been used a lot since then.

Hispanic composers have undoubtedly met with much success in the classical music world. As I pointed out, they have written in every style in the classical music repertoire. Rodrigo's *Concierto de Aranjuez* (1939), for instance, has been played more than any other concerto for guitar in recent years. Brazilian Hector Villa-Lobos (Brazil 1887-1959) also spread it around and churned out works in many forms. He really hit it big, though, when he paid homage to Bach with a huge taste of Brazil mixed into his ever-popular *Bachianas Brasileiras (Brazilian Bachian)* pieces on concert bills that he composed between 1930 and 1945; this is recognized and acclaimed as among the most important instrumental works ever written. At the same time, like black composers, they have infused classical music with the unique style and sounds of their own national cultures. This, in and of itself, has evolved classical music into a truly global, multi-cultural experience that can be shared and enjoyed by all peoples.

As mentioned previously, many owe a huge debt to Bach and Handel and the other greats of the Baroque period. Haydn, Mozart, and Beethoven are absolutely the top cats, the names everyone thinks of when the subject of classical music comes up, rightly so. Volumes have been written on these greats, but my discussion should be viewed as merely my personal impression, admiration, and a capsulated add-on to and about them.

Franz Joseph Haydn

CHAPTER 5

A Guide to the Three Giants

"For some time I was quite beside myself over his (Mozart's) death, and could not believe that Providence should so quickly have called away an irreplaceable man into the next world."

—Franz Joseph Haydn

I have no doubt that thousands of filmgoers got their first introduction to Mozart in 1984, through the thoroughly ribald, slightly goofball, and mostly fabricated but still delightful *Amadeus.* My wife and I saw it three times, and each time, we did something we've almost never done at movies: We sat stock still in our seats, mesmerized by the second movement of Mozart's *Piano Concerto No. 20* (1785) as it played as the backdrop to the film's ending credits.

Almost anything that can be said, written, and even shown on the big screen about Wolfgang Amadeus Mozart (Germany, 1756-91) has been, said, written, and shown. On the other hand, there's no quasi bio-pic on his one-time teacher and ardent champion, Papa Haydn, aka Franz Joseph

Haydn (Germany, 1732-1809). Nevertheless, he's no piker when it comes to the volume of words that have penned about him and his music alike. The reason for this is simple: Unquestionably, they are two unchallenged giants of the mid- to late eighteenth century classical music.

Encore

AMADEUS II ANYONE?

Amadeus was a stark example of Hollywood having great fun while taking lots of creative liberty when it came to the life of a historic figure; as is often the case with the movers and shakers in movie town, spicing up his life a bit was deemed a necessity in order to pack the theaters. The irony is that Mozart's life was anything but that of the stereotyped dry, boring, musician-composer. Contrary to the silver screen rendition, the real Amadeus wasn't poor, childlike with a high, cackling voice; poisoned; or dumped into a pauper's grave as depicted in the motion picture. He was, however, a child prodigy, a show-stopper, and a trickster with and on the piano. The consummate partier, he also gambled, shot pool, was once cursed out by an archbishop, cavorted with an assortment of on-the-make musical hustlers and ne'er-do-wells, often sold his music for an exorbitant amount of money, then lived the high life with his profits. Even his deathbed was teeming with drama fit for any screenplay, when a mysterious stranger commissioned him to write *The Requiem*. That stranger

was a count who wanted to pawn the piece off as his own, a forgery for which he stood to make a fortune. Mozart's memorial service in Prague on December 14, 1791 was a dramatic, moving affair, with thousands flocking to the streets and belting out a chorus of boo-hoos over the music supplied by some of the city's best musicians. Truly, Amadeus did not capture the real fun and drama of the real man's life, worthy of any blockbuster, so maybe there is call for a sequel.

Since this is a beginner's guide to classical music, I feel I am obliged to add something here. Both Mozart and Haydn spawned a growth industry in pop, film, and even elevator Muzak. They wrote, refined, amplified, expanded, and even brought and used new creative and innovative techniques, styles, forms, and instrumentation to Western music. Each composed in the following forms: operas, sonatas, keyboard and violin trios and quartets, piano (Mozart and Haydn), violin concertos (Mozart), bassoon, flute, clarinet concertos (Mozart) and trumpet and cello concertos (Haydn), and sacred masses. The four large musical forms composed by both included symphonies, concertos, masses, and opera.

* * * * *

Every musicologist, breathing and non-breathing, has talked about how Haydn's and Mozart's symphonies were foundational for each other and for the giants of the nineteenth-century classical music from Beethoven to Brahms.

Just consider the instruments they used. Haydn and Mozart scored their symphonies for oboes, horns, trombones, flutes, bassoons, violins, bass, cellos, drums, clarinets, and occasionally trumpets. Both wrote their symphonies in what became the standard four-movement work. As previously noted, this usually consists of a fast opening, a slow movement, and a fast finale. Don't forget that they are big on the minuet too; got to get the dance in there!

From My Concert Seat

I love to watch conductors move through the musical scores in front of them on the podium as they conduct. Some lightly turn the pages, while others flip them furiously. Some don't bother with score books at all. The score book shows how the notes, instruments, and voices line up in a composition. It is large enough for the conductor to study before rehearsal and to read while directing rehearsals and performances. The next time you attend a concert, keep an eye on the flippin' conductor!

To make a point about Haydn's technique, we can turn to his *Symphony No. 92, "The Oxford."* I first heard this played by a local college orchestra. When I read *"Oxford"* in the program, I actually thought it was the famed college in England, the one Haydn was writing music about; needless to say, that was in my earlier days of attending to classical concerts. For the record, he actually wrote it in 1789, as one of a set of three symphonies a French count paid him to write, along with a request by some Bavarian nobles for some new music. First and foremost, business is business.

In the first movement of the symphony, there is point and counterpoint. The second movement is slow. The third comprises stylized minuets (dancing again), with the first repeated after the second. The final movement roars home. Haydn used the rondo form to close his symphonies. Above all, he wanted his symphonies to leave the listener with a high-spirited, good feeling; thus, their spirited closing.

In listening to other Haydn symphonies with such fun nicknames as, "*The Bear,*" "*The Philosopher,*" "*The Hen,*" "*The Military,*" "*The Drumroll,*" "*The Miracle,*" "*The Surprise,*" "*The Clock*" and "*Maria Theresa,*" I'm always struck by the wit, color, lyricism, and just plain fun he had in and with those symphonies.

I'm amazed every time I look at Haydn's output. It is beyond gargantuan; 104 officially or 106 or even 108 symphonies, depending on the source; 68 string quartets; 47 piano sonatas; 26 operas; 4 oratorios; and several hundred fiddling-around, smaller pieces. Though many were lost, strayed, or just overstayed their welcome, there's always been more than enough Haydn to fill up any orchestra concert bill for decades. I can certainly vouch for that, since many orchestras and concerts I have attended have been headlined by one or another of Haydn's symphonies.

From My Concert Seat

I long wondered why Haydn wrote so many symphonies—100-plus—when Beethoven only wrote 9, Brahms 4, and Mozart 41. Haydn certainly didn't need the money, right? Well, truthfully, that's not necessarily accurate. He wrote them because he was paid to; he was the official composer of the wealthy Prince Esterhazy. The prince hosted many festive events that required lots of music. Since Haydn was on the prince's payroll, he had to do his job, and that meant writing.

Recommended Listening

F.J. Haydn, *Trumpet Concerto in E Flat Major*

Encore

NICKNAMING A HAYDN SYMPHONY

Haydn's *Symphony No. 82,* popularly known as *"The Bear,"* was a symphony commissioned for a Paris premiere in 1786. History does not know this simply his *Symphony No. 82;* of the official 104 symphonies Haydn wrote, that would have got lost in the deluge of other numbered symphonies, so someone got creative with it. Often, that someone was an enterprising publisher or agent, people who could see a bigger pile of guilders, pounds, or francs

in slapping a catchy nickname on a composer's work. Thus, in time, Haydn's *Symphony No. 82* became something far more memorable as *"The Bear."* Since one can't just slap any old name on a symphony to make the marketing gimmick work, there had to be a tie-in, rather real or stretched, to the work. In *No. 82* the tie-in was a repeating feature in the last movement; the instruments used seemed to spark a visual of dancing bears, popular crowd entertainment of the era.

Aside from the nickname of the symphony, there is another memorable note to it. The man at the podium directing the *Concert de la Loge Olympique* at its premier in 1787 was Chevalier de Saint-Georges, one of France's most celebrated conductors—and he was black.

I marvel when I read accounts of the almost father-son relationship between Haydn and Mozart. In fact, at times, it was far better than the relation between Mozart and his musician-composer-teacher-promoter real father, Leopold Mozart. (Germany, 1719-87). The elder Mozart's *Cassation in G Major,* better known as *"Toy Symphony,"* is fun listening as well, albeit with a nickname like that, it couldn't be anything but. Papa Mozart was the one who launched his wunderkind son's career. When Wolfgang was small, the boy, along with his sister, who was nicknamed Nannerl, was trotted all over Europe in an effort to showcase his virtuoso magic. As such, the relationship between father and son was sometimes strained by the demands of the tour. As an adult, the certified genius wanted to go his own way, as so many young people do, and that was exactly what he did.

* * * * *

Mozart had to show his admiration and appreciation for Haydn, and there was no better way than to write music, especially dedicated to him. He published them as a set of string instrument quartets in 1785. Since it was Haydn whose symphonies had a penchant for attracting nicknames, so did three of the quartets: "*Spring,*" "*Hunt,*" and "*Dissonance.*" Haydn's influence on Mozart turned up in what many regard as Mozart's last and greatest symphony, *Symphony No. 41 in C Major,* K. 551 (1788), the one the musical world knows as "*The Jupiter.*" The nickname had nothing to do with the planet and everything to do with clever marketing by his London publisher.

The similarity between the opening theme of one of Haydn's earliest symphonies, *Symphony No. 13 in D Major* (1763) and that of the first movement of "*The Jupiter*" is too noticeable to be pure coincidence.

"K." *Short for "Kochel listing." This is Ludwig von Köchel's arrangement and cataloging of Mozart's works in chronological order.*

I know many consider Mozart's operas his strong suit; however, his concertos might be able to lay claim. They were written in three movements, fast-slow-fast, with the second movement often sounding like a lyrical opera or aria. No surprise there, given Mozart's genius with and absolute command of the operatic form. Mozart included cadenzas in most of his piano concertos. They give the soloist an opportunity to improvise and shine. Mozart was always careful that the solo piano parts didn't overshadow the orchestra.

I can almost see him putting his dainty, feather-like pen to paper in his one clarinet concerto, bassoon concerto, four horn concertos, and five violin concertos. They are tight and economical, with the same genteel touch in their sound as Mozart's earlier piano concertos. This makes sense, since he wrote the clarinet concerto, bassoon concerto, and the horn concertos specifically as performance pieces for his musician friends. The violin concertos may also have been set pieces for the orchestra he conducted while in the pay of the archbishop of Salzberg (1773-76).

From My Concert Seat

I wasn't surprised that a couple hundred years after Mozart wrote his clarinet concerto, Hollywood came calling. The dreamlike, soft strains of the second movement waft against the expansive rolling scenery of East Africa in the 1985 hit, *Out of Africa.* Some say it was Mozart rather than Meryl Streep or Robert Redford that made the film, and I would agree. To this day, it is the only thing I can remember from the film.

Recommended Listening

W.A. Mozart, *The Violin Concerto No. 5 in A Major "The Turkish" and Clarinet Concerto in A Major*

As I said, I've listened countless times to Mozart piano concertos. I am always struck by their light touch, charm, and elegance. More than that, they are just plain fun to listen to, and that comes through in the music. I must confess, though, that it took some time for me to fully appreciate the sheer beauty, flow, and youthful innocence of Mozart's music. I was originally a Beethoven and Tchaikovsky guy, as I reveled in the sheer power, blast, and the big bang, martial beat of Tchaikovsky's *Fifth Symphony* or Beethoven's *Third Symphony.*

Two things changed that for me. One was the 1967 Swedish film, *Elvira Madigan,* in which I heard the transcendent, ethereal second movement of the music that made it famous. Mozart's piece was promptly tagged in popular listening with *"Elvira Madigan,"* but the official name was *Piano Concerto No. 21* (1785).

The other thing that got my attention was my wife, Barbara. She is absolutely wild about Mozart, and listening to it so much because of her and with her sealed the deal.

Encore

A Musical Joke

Mozart had a ribald, apparently sardonic sense of humor. Though he did not make a habit of putting down the works of other composers, he apparently scorned some of the bad composing of his day. The only composer Mozart ever publicly praised was Haydn, as you might have guessed. "He alone," Wolfgang said, "has the secret of making me smile and touching me to the bottom of my soul." That's pretty heady stuff, but it was also remarkably true.

Through the years, there has been endless speculation, and it is believed that one of the reasons he wrote *A Musical Joke (Ein musikalischer Spaß)* K. 522, (divertimento for two horns and string quartet) in 1787 was to show how bad some of the writing actually was. He deliberately jumbled notes, harmony, and rhythm to produce a riotous, odd-sounding piece. We'll never really know Mozart's exact motives for composing such a musical jumble. It's still fun to listen to, if for no other reason than even Mozart at his worse is still Mozart at his best.

Recommended Listening

W.A. Mozart, *Great Mass in C Major*

* * * * *

I can't begin to imagine what a pain in the drain it must have been for Haydn to try to corral the twenty-year-old, headstrong Beethoven during the year or so while Haydn was his teacher. Still, Haydn and Mozart created a bridge to Beethoven. The teacher-student relationship Haydn had with him was doomed, as Beethoven just had too many ideas of his own on how and what he wanted to write. The seeds of the rupture purportedly came over what Haydn wanted Beethoven to insert in his compositions, the Op. 1 (opus is a work) piano trios: the phrase "pupil of Haydn" to help Beethoven better market his product. Beethoven balked at this. It didn't help the relationship when Haydn suggested that Beethoven not publish one of the trios. There were other spats too. Beethoven soon went his way with a famously quoted dig, stating he didn't learn anything from Haydn. However, he remained respectful toward him, at least publicly, and even later in life, he spoke highly of him.

To be charitable, Beethoven was disingenuous in his privately uttered, dim view of Haydn. He owed him a lot. The most cursory listen to his *Symphony No. 1* (1801) (and *No. 2)* (1801-02) bears the direct stamp of both Haydn and Mozart. As in both of the master's works, they're the paragon of elegant simplicity and exude fun and energy. Yet Beethoven was still Beethoven, and in spots, he departed in spots. There is a slow but jarring introduction, thoughtful, and reflective interludes and dance like passages.

Beethoven was also not averse to fleshing out his works with material from other sources. My favorite, the *Seventh Symphony*, is a case in point. The third movement carries an unmistakable melody that Beethoven scholars say was lifted from the pilgrims' hymn of lower Austria; if it was useful and worked, it made sense to incorporate. Composers did it all the time, and Beethoven was no different.

From My Concert Seat

I never thought any composer could just scribble down on paper a concerto or a symphony off the top of his or her head, even in some blinding flash of inspiration, and that includes Mozart and definitely Beethoven. He was a genius, to be sure, but to bring that genius to fruition and create works for the ages requires a lot of time and sweat. His masterworks did not come in a blinding flash of inspiration. His sketchbooks tell a story of a man who wrote, rewrote, scratched out, penciled in, penciled out, erased, and revised, revised, and revised some more to work out his ideas until he got it just right.

I have often heard in concert his first two symphonies, which are always said to be almost carbon copies of the Haydn-Mozart style. To an extent, they are; however, Beethoven was clearly on a mission to take the symphony to the next level. His aim was to transform it from delicate, entertaining, or even light fare to a powerful vehicle of dramatic musical expression. This meant adding more time, more minutes, to the symphony. This, in turn, meant greatly expanding the length of a symphony to pack a wallop, and it allowed him to develop the intense, heart-churning ideas he sought to express. You've probably heard the *dum-dum-de-dum* opening notes in his *Symphony No. 5* (1804-08), somewhere along the line, even if you've never listened to a symphony.

From My Concert Seat

In one week in April of 2006, I heard the same Beethoven symphony played by the Los Angeles Philharmonic Orchestra and a local community orchestra. In both cases, I was struck by the drama of the sound. I thought of the characters, the action, and the power of performance that came through in the playing. It was so overwhelming, like being hit by a musical freight train. I jumped to my feet in giddy applause at both concerts.

Recommended Listening

L.V. Beethoven, *Violin Concerto in D Major*

I can't tell you how many lines have been written on Beethoven's *Symphony No. 3, "The Eroica"* (1804). It is always regarded as the symphony that stood the classical music world on its head. It shattered all previous conventions in the symphonic genre. Still, I think another reason there's so much talk about it is because of what he did with its name. By all the political standards of the day, Beethoven was considered a radical Democrat or anti-royalist. The oft-told story is that Beethoven so admired Napoleon that he intended to dedicate this symphony to him. As the story goes, Napoleon upset that apple cart by declaring himself emperor. A furious Beethoven angrily crossed Napoleon's name off the manuscript, as contemporaries say, but that ripped-out name still supposedly can be seen on the original today.

Encore

I TAKE IT ALL BACK

Sinfonia Eroica (1804): The title page shows Beethoven's erasure of his dedication of the work to Napoleon Bonaparte.

"The Eroica" (heroic) is big, powerful, long, sweeping, dynamic, and, as its name implies, even heroic—maybe even Olympian—in stature. The movements in various order are: project challenge, struggle, and final victory. The pathos is conveyed in the funeral march, and Beethoven's belief in the freedom and egalitarianism of the French Revolution and Napoleon, whom, as I said, Beethoven ultimately felt betrayed the ideal. It comes through in the fanfare and drum rolls, which sound like a revolutionary march and hymn. The symphony both engaged and challenged listeners in a way no other symphony before or since have done. Rather than just pure entertainment, it was a work of deep thought, expression, and humanitarian ideals.

From My Concert Seat

I once called the conductor of the UCLA Philharmonic Orchestra, a friend, to tell him to give an ol' pat on the back to his drummer after a performance of *"The Eroica"* symphony, because his fantastic drumming gave it even more of a jolt. It was so hard, and he was in such a zone that I wondered if he thought he was hitting his licks on Beethoven or the Red Hot Chili Peppers.

"The Eroica" may be the gold standard as the symphony that changed everything. Still, as I made amply clear in my introduction to this book, I personally think his *Symphony*

No. 7, which he sometimes called his favorite, and *No. 9,* the choral symphony, are both groundbreaking in form, tempo, and style. In addition, the use of text, poetry, and the choral in his *Symphony No. 9* is an electrifying affirmation of the sheer power of sound.

Still *"The Eroica"* is considered a high mark in the radical evolution of the symphony because it was the first to do the things that critics credit it with doing: to shake up the classical music world with its massive sound and length. By piling in even more instruments than were typically used by composers and heard by concert audiences, he made it truly titanic.

There's a final happy note to the Beethoven-Haydn approach avoidance tryst. It came when a dying Haydn was carried in on a chair to a performance of his oratorio masterwork, *The Creation,* in 1808. Beethoven was there, and without missing a beat, he strode over to the chair and kissed Haydn's hands and forehead. It had to be a touching moment, and it was not lost on some who had heard Beethoven's sometimes disparaging remarks about Haydn; undoubtedly, they knew nothing of the private high regard he really did harbor for him.

Recommended Listening

L.V. Beethoven, *The Missa Solemnis in D Major*

* * * * *

It's difficult for me to believe that Beethoven and Mozart were religious men. Haydn openly spoke of praying night and day to ask God to give him strength to finish his works. Mozart and Beethoven, however, are a different story. The tales of Mozart's penchant for games, risqué jokes, and a devil-may-care attitude, as well as Beethoven's with his rages and legendary cantankerousness, belie the image of men who knew how to keep and praise God in their own way, let alone put God on display in their music. However, Mozart's sacred masses, most notably his *Great Mass in C Minor* (1782-83) and *The Requiem Mass in D Minor* (1791) and Beethoven's mass, *Missa Solemnis* (1819-23) and oratorio, *Christus am Ölberge (Christ on the Mount of Olives)* (1802) are phenomenal, reverberatingly spiritual works for choir, orchestra, and solo singers.

One of the best renditions of Mozart's *Great Mass* was performed by the New West Symphony Orchestra in May of 2015 in Santa Monica. The soloists and chorale were stirring, lively, and movingly passionate. I like to think Wolfgang would have loved every moment of it.

These works are warmly engaging in spirit and stand as rapturous hymns of praise to God and the heavens; however, it was Haydn who took the sacred mass and oratorio to the upper limits of the stratosphere. He made it clear that he simply had to have one final work that would express his everlasting gratitude to the creator. The work he had in mind would be called just that, a three-part wonder known as *The Creation,* based on the creation of the world as described in the Book of Genesis and John Milton's *Paradise Lost.* An aging and increasingly infirmed Haydn was determined to finish that work before the clock on his life ran out. As the story goes, he was down on his knees again, praying hard for time to finish that one final great work, a swan song that would be his testament to the ages, to God, and to the universe at large. "I knelt down every day and prayed God to strengthen me for my work," he said, and God apparently did.

Encore

The Creation

The first public performance of *The Creation* was at Vienna's old Burgtheater in 1799, though a private one was held a year earlier. Haydn was present at the public one, and that ensured that it was an event not to be missed. Understandably, it was sold out, far in advance. In fact, the demand to see it was so great that it was performed nearly forty more times in Vienna while he was alive. In 1808, the year before his death, Haydn attended one last performance. He had to be carried in to the theater on an armchair, to a round of thunderous applause. Haydn weakly pointed a finger up and said, "Not from me. Everything comes from up there!"

Recommended Listening

F.J. Haydn, *Lord Nelson Mass in D. Minor*

I could never call Haydn, Mozart, or Beethoven a one-trick pony, for they also wrote operas. Haydn wrote a dozen or more of them, though these are seldom ever performed today. Unfortunately, Beethoven, he stayed with only one: his *Fidelio,* one he kept tinkering with. The final two-act version of that opera enjoyed a respectable reception when it premiered in 1805 and has received some modest acclaim in the decades hence. As mentioned earlier, overtures sometimes live on long after the operas they come from bite the dust, and it was no different for Beethoven's opera. The overture he toyed with has been played to death, while the opera is simply an occasional stage work.

Mozart never had to worry about that fate, for his operatic works, large and small, have comprised the yardstick by which all opera is measured since the ink dried on his first major one, *Idomeneo* (1780).

The old masters recognized that opera was where the audiences and money would be, but opera was also a way for them to stretch out and tell or retell a good tale. This was and always has been the biggest challenge and fascination for countless composers, the reason why so many try their hand at opera. There have been as many failures as successes though. I cite one disaster of an opera opening in the next chapter, but in that case, the composer had the last laugh.

Now for my last detour from the old masters. I have already mentioned one woman, Barbara Strozzi, who shook up the good ol' boys' club during the early Baroque period by writing dozens of secular vocal songs, but she was the very rare exception. There is a particular shame in the fact that while the cloak of invisibility has been drawn tight over black composers and somewhat less over Hispanic composers, female composers have been virtually hidden behind the veil. It's been an uphill fight for them to receive any acknowledgment, as if it is inconceivable that a woman is even capable of composing. For this reason, it took me years to discover that there were women like Strozzi and others who did wage a fight for recognition, but they do deserve a place in the pages of this book.

Barbara Strozzi

CHAPTER 6

A Guide to Women Classical Composers

"It must be a sign of talent that I do not give up, though I can get nobody to take an interest in my efforts."
—Fanny Mendelssohn Hensel

One line in a short essay that examines the role of women in the world of classical music put it quite charitably, though it is one of the greatest understatements of all time: "The role of women composers in the evolution of classical music is often underappreciated." Classical music composers of African ancestry have been mostly invisible in the literature for two centuries. Hispanic composers have fared much better, though they are still considered only the second string of classical composers. The brutal reality, though, is that female composers seem vaguely nonexistent.

I liken women in classical music to distance runner Kathrine Switzer. An official attempted to yank her from the 1967 Boston Marathon, and one official later explained, "Women can't run in the Marathon because the rules forbid it." Unlike her, though, in nearly all cases, women in classical music have not gotten to the classical music start line. The handful who have saw their would-be careers smacked down before they barely inched forward on the classical music road.

There is no subtlety about the impregnable barrier women have crashed against, for classical music composing has been strictly the domain of males. It didn't matter how much creative or musical talent exploded from the head or the pen of a woman; she was quickly shunned or even reviled for even trying. Mozart's older sister, Maria Anna Mozart, Nannerl, (Germany, 1751-1829) is a timeless example of the plight of talented eighteenth-century ladies. Her story was told in the partly fictionalized film, *Mozart's Sister* (2010). She was a first-rate pianist and almost certainly could have been a first-rate composer if given a tenth of a chance. Mozart wrote several compositions for her to perform, including *Prelude and Fugue in C,* K. 394 (1782) and sent her copies of his piano concertos. In that era, motherhood and child-rearing and being a good, dutiful helpmate to her husband was her proscribed lot in life, and that was the life to which she eventually dutifully resigned herself.

From My Concert Seat

I have attended nearly 500 concerts in the past twenty years, from 1995 to 2015. In these two decades, among all those grand performances, I have seen a grand total of two female conductors on the podium during that time. I have heard no works performed by a female composer.

I made it a special point to attend concerts by one of the two female conductors, Lucinda Carver in the mid- to late 1990s. For a while, Lucinda expertly conducted her own group, the Los Angeles Mozart Orchestra. Unfortunately, the orchestra didn't last. I still have the Mozart t-shirt I bought at one of the concerts. For now, that small souvenir will have to do to keep the memory alive of Carver conducting an orchestra.

As in many cases in history, a propensity for discrimination against gender and race stymied, stifled, and flattened enormous musical talent and genius. I can only lament what musically inclined women of the day might have accomplished if the doors had been open to them.

Recommended Listening

Fanny Mendelssohn, *Notturno in G Minor*

* * * * *

I need not speculate about the best-known nineteenth-century female composer-musician, Clara Schumann (Germany, 1819-96). She is sometimes touted as the woman who slightly broke through the barrier of the gender-barred classical music club, and she somehow overcame great odds and managed to carve out a successful concert stage career. However, in reality, she isn't totally the exception. She did get acclaim, but that was mostly because of her last name, Schumann, and her husband, Robert. She also got lucky and later had a close professional association—and maybe romantic one as well—with Brahms.

Schumann deeply appreciated her and recognized her monster piano virtuosity. He showcased it whenever and wherever he could, and he heeded her advice, encouragement, and suggestions in writing his symphony and his *Piano Concerto in A Minor* (1845), which Clara made one of her signature performance pieces. Still, she had no illusions about her place in the classical music world then: "I once believed that I possessed creative talent, but I have given up this idea; a woman must not desire to compose... There has never yet been one able to do it. Should I expect to be the one?"

Robert, however, didn't always cast an eye over her shoulder when it came to performing and composing.

One of her main instrumental works, *Trio for Violin, Cello, and Piano,* Op. 17 (1846) is fresh, light, dainty, yet intensely passionate, with a subtle grace and power that captivates. There is a slight stamp of Robert on it, in its lyrical passages; however, the piece departs quickly and takes on a colorful sound of its own.

From My Concert Seat

If you want to hear the works of female composers then and now, *YouTube* can be a blessing. Without this medium, we would know even less about their music.

Every chance I get, I listen to excerpts from female composers such as Clara Schumann and Florence Price, and it's great listening. I suspect more would listen to them if they knew about them. Now that you do, give them a listen!

Recommended Listening

Clara Schumann, Piano Concerto, Op. 7 in A Minor

If one woman got a brief pass from the no-girls-allowed club, it was the sister of the other classical music giant, Felix Mendelsohn. Fanny (Germany, 1805-47) was even more prolific than Clara. She wrote over 460 pieces of music, several books of solo piano pieces and songs, a cycle of pieces depicting the months of the year, *Das Jahr (The Year)* (1840), and her well-crafted *Piano Trio* (1846). Many of her songs would have had more chance of seeing snow in the tropics than seeing the light of publishing print if brother Felix hadn't lent his name to it and published them in his *Opus 8* and *9* collections.

Even Felix's involvement didn't guarantee that someone wouldn't mix up the two "F's," Fanny for Felix, and that was exactly what happened during one of Felix's much-acclaimed visits to London's Buckingham Palace, where he was to be received and entertained by Queen Victoria. Vicky occasionally liked to belt out a tune or two and show off her musical prowess.

Encore

WHICH MENDELSSOHN?

On July 9, 1842, Queen Victoria wrote in her diary, "Mendelssohn came to take leave of Albert, previous to his returning to Germany, and he was good enough to play for us, on Albert's organ, which he did beautifully. As he wished to hear me sing, we took him over to the large room, where, with some trepidation, I sang, accompanied by him, first a song which I thought was his composition but which he said was his sister's and then one of his beautiful ones, after which he played to us a little. We thanked him very much, and I gave him a handsome ring as a remembrance."

* * * * *

I often hear that the one and only exception was Amy Marcy Cheney Beach (America, 1867-1944). She was also the requisite wife and mother, but she managed to step out of that role and take her career in hand. She hit the big and the little concert stages whenever the opportunity presented itself. In her one and only concerto, the *Piano Concerto,* Op. 45 (1899), Beach combined the passionate lyricism of European Post-Romanticism with the blues and folk style of American music. If not for *YouTube.* I probably wouldn't have heard her anywhere either.

Her work has been branded as the first "feminist" work

for piano, with its thumping notes that seemed to bellow out in open rebellion against the piano offerings of, say, George Gershwin and the like. Beach herself premiered it in 1900. In doing so, she ushered in a new century in which women, like men, would be recognized as leaders in musical composition. Considering the age in which she worked, she does seem to be the one true exception to the exclusionary rule.

In November of 2014, The British Academy of Songwriters, Composers, and Arrangers sponsored a unique panel in London. The panel consisted of seven composers, all female. They talked about their experiences in the classical music world. As they did, they pulled no punches and lambasted the classical music arena for still being very much a man's world. One panelist, Composer Judith Bingham, revealed that she kept numbers on just how many pieces by women London's major classical music radio stations played. "If you're lucky, there may be one. Sometimes, there's nothing," she lamented. "It's like women just don't exist."

They do and they don't. Those seven female composers are living proof that women are composing good music and lots of it. The big difference between modern day and decades prior is these ladies are willing to raise their voices everywhere to make sure their music is heard. Those voices will get louder and louder until the age-old gender-based barrier comes crashing down in the classical music world, once and for all.

From My Concert Seat

I have personally seen one other magnificent exception to the general invisibility of women on the conductor's podium. Sonia Marie De Leon de Vega has been knocking them dead for years with her fiery, explosive conducting of the orchestra she founded, the Santa Cecilia Orchestra. I have followed her work closely through the years. She has made it her special mission to steer thousands, if not tens of thousands, of Latino, young, and not-so-young listeners into classical music halls. She knew it wouldn't be easy, and she was right about that. "Because you can deprive people of this, put up barriers and say, 'This is elitist. This is not for you.' Because we have no music in our schools and communities, you can't expect people to be there. I knew I had to build our audience literally one family at a time. I thought, *If I can't get the adults here, I'll get the children here,* so I went to schools." The children? Brilliant, for today, her concerts are not just concerts but events. She's more than proven that if you put the music out there and stay with it, classical music can indeed break down the barriers.

But I can't leave it at that, for a wave of both new and seasoned modern-day female composers are making their mark in the field. As with the Hispanic and black composers, they've composed in many of the major musical forms, all while tossing in a lot of creative innovation along the way.

* * * * *

Gender aside for a moment, one composer who has to rank at or near the top of the perch of the most prolific of the present-day composers is Jamaican-born Eleanor Alberga. She has guest conducted for London's Royal Academy of Music, and her works have been performed by the Royal Philharmonic, the London Philharmonic, Bournemouth Sinfonietta, London Mozart Players, and the Women's Philharmonic of San Francisco. She has written operas, a violin concerto, string quartets, piano suites, and vocal chamber works. Cheryl Frances-Hoad has won numerous top composer awards, and her *Five Rackets for Trio Relay* has gotten much acclaim. Dobrinka Tabakova's *String Paths* have gotten a Grammy award nomination. One of the works in the cycle is *Suite in Old Style,* which features viola, harpsichord, and strings that mix in folk music, dance, and Eastern sounds. Charlotte Bray has won raves for her orchestral work, *At the Speed of Stillness;* it plays off some of the music of Benjamin Britten, with much of her own unique musical interpretation.

Meredith Monk is one of the older names among contemporary women composers. One of her principal works, *Songs for Ascension* blends the traditional classical form with the avant garde styling harmonies and wordless vocal writing. Anna Clyne's *Masquerade* has been performed by several orchestras. Then there are the many works of Joan Tower, one of which is the playfully titled, *Fanfare for the Uncommon*

Woman, an in-your-face musical jibe at Aaron Copland's popular *Fanfare for the Common Man*. Tower's ***Fanfare*** combines driving rhythms with lilting and soft, easy harmonies. Other prominent modern-day female composers who have made and are making their presence felt are Ruth Crawford Seeger, Gabriela Lena frank, and Kaijo Saariaho.

Again, these are just a very few of the new and seasoned talents among female classical music composers, and many more will follow. That said, I think a good segue from my look at the near invisibility of women as composers and even performers in the classical music world is to now return to an area of classical music in which many women have made their mark, an area that has garnered much well-deserved fanfare over time: the world of opera. I discussed the earlier opera masters of the Baroque period. Now we'll look at the big opera guns of the nineteenth century, whose names and works are best known today.

CHAPTER 7

A Guide to Opera

"Eating, loving, singing, and digesting are, in truth, the four acts of the comic opera known as life, and they pass like bubbles of a bottle of champagne. Whoever lets them break without having enjoyed them is a complete fool."

—Giaochimo Rossini

A good Italian-American friend once mockingly referred to opera as "the scourge of the Italian nation." He was an avid jazz lover, so for him, music began and ended with Charley Parker, Miles Davis, and John Coltrane. While I delighted in listening to symphonies, concertos, masses, and, later, all forms of chamber music, I just couldn't get his derisive put-down of opera out of my head.

From My Concert Seat

In September of 2003, the L.A. Opera Company premiered Deborah Drattell's *Nicholas and Alexandra,* a production is based on the ill-fated life of Russian Czar Nicholas and his wife, murdered by the Bolsheviks in 1918. It was one long gab-fest, a real bore. My eyes were glued to

my watch the entire time, and I longed for intermission so I could make my escape. At that point, I thought my friend's assessment about opera was spot on. Based on what I saw and heard that day, he'd nailed it.

Regardless of his harsh critique and the tragedy of the tragedy I grueling sat through, I didn't give up on opera and decided to give it one more try, with the Los Angeles Opera Company staging of Mozart's *Magic Flute.* It was aptly titled, as something magical did happen. It was like Beethoven's *Seventh Symphony* all over again; it was utterly majestic and affected me as only Mozart could. It pulsed with melting sound, festive movement, and exhilarating life. Grown as I was, I was like a kid in a play land as I watched and listened, mesmerized and tingling with delight. In short, it was magical to hear.

It was that performance that forced me to rethink my classical musical interest and education. I simply had to get into opera. Since more volumes have been written on opera than even the symphony, and since I now know where I'm going with it, I'll stick with the basics of opera.

I'll start with bel canto, a brand new way of writing for the voice from the old Baroque style. It literally translates to "beautiful voice." Opera without beautiful singing would be like trying to play basketball without the hoop. The singing showcases technique, style, and tone and emphasizes the singer's vocal range, flexibility, agility, and command of melodies. That's a lot to pack into a human voice, but it is a requirement of opera. Gioachino Rossini; Vincenzo Bellini (Italy, 1801-35), *Norma* (1831); and Gaetano Donizetti (Italy, 1797-1848), *Don Pasquale* (1843); were three of the best-known Italian operatic composers, and they played up beautiful singing big time in their operas.

Of course these weren't the only ones. A German, Carl Maria von Weber (1786-1826), did the same thing in his large-scale work, *Der Freischütz (The Free-Shooter)* (1821). Weber gleaned the idea for this opera from the same place where legions of other opera composers have traditionally taken theirs from: He simply looked around and found an old story and song that had been kicking around for years. For Weber, it was an old German folk song and legend. He packed his production with ghosts, magic bullets, hellhounds, and lots of bargaining with the devil. It's yet another opera with a knockout of an overture played incessantly, while the opera has been relegated almost to a passing footnote in the opera repertoire. The times I've heard it played in concert, I have tried to visualize the ghosts and goblins scampering around on the operatic stage, and the powerful performance makes for vivid imaginings.

Recommended Listening

C.M. Von Weber, *Overture to Der Freischütz, Op. 77*

Encore

WHEN MEN BECAME WOMEN

In the early days, the opera stage exhibited a kind of perverse gender poetic justice. Women were strictly forbidden to sing any of the high-pitched alto and soprano roles; however, it looked and sounded a bit peculiar with only deeper male tenor and bass voices. Opera guys found a way around it: Boys sang the higher parts. The problem was that as those boys grew into men, their voices changed and deepened.

The solution was painfully simple, and I do mean painfully. Opera singers that became known as the *castrati* were castrated before they hit puberty. This stopped nature in its tracks, physiologically freezing the boy's development, a larynx interrupted, if you will. Needless to say, in time, this arcane practice was stopped. Modern enlightenment prevailed, and it was discovered that women can actually sing alto and soprano. In 1870, Italy declared castration for singing illegal, so the practice mercifully ended.

I find it almost embarrassing to mention this about Bellini and Donizetti, but the reality is that they are almost bare footnotes in opera as compared to the composer who has set the mark for Italian opera for more than a century. Giuseppe Verdi (Italy 1813-1901) was yet another in the long train of classical child musical prodigies. At age eight, he was hired as a paid organist at his local church. Over the years that followed, he began writing small works for organ and piano, both of which he played at concerts. It does take time for one to find his or her true calling, even for the greats. After extensive training and conservatory stints, Verdi finally found his, a calling that would change the face of music yet again. His first opera, *Oberto* (1839) received some stage play. His second full-blown stage piece, *Un Giorno di Regno* (1840) was a flop. He soon overcame whatever self-doubt he had about his ability to compose operas. The result was the wildly successful *Nabucco,* and just like that, Verdi was now off and running.

In relatively quick succession, he composed twenty more operas, or, as he put it in a letter in 1858, "From *Nabucco* (1842), a big hit, you may say, I have never had one hour of peace. Sixteen years in the galleys." Some of his greatest and best-known operas, such as *Rigoletto, Il Trovatore* and *La Traviata,* hit the stage in the years known as his "middle period," the 1850s. *Aida* was really his runaway smash hit in the later years; it is a fixture on opera stages worldwide today.

Verdi did not depart an inch from the *bel canto* style in his early operas. It was a proven model for success for the opera-composing luminaries of the day, so there was no point in fixing something that was not broken. Nevertheless, as Verdi's star continued to rise, he stretched, fleshed out, and experimented with style, harmony, and orchestration. This unique spin, this stretching of traditional boundaries, is what gives his works such a distinctive character and the accolades his operas have rightfully received as highly individual, dramatic works of art. Verdi also proved that opera is a big deal for the masses.

From My Concert Seat

From time to time, I've heard classical music radio station announcers mention that Verdi's funeral in 1901 was practically a State affair in Italy, complete with lots of singing. I try to picture his memorial service every time I hear the *Va Pinsiero,* better known as *"The Chorus of the Hebrew Slaves"* from his opera *Nabucco,* and it is played a lot. This little number was played at his funeral, and the thousands of folks who mobbed the streets of Milan to hail him burst out in spontaneous singing of the tune.

Recommended Listening

G. Donizetti, *An Introduction to Donizetti's L'elisir d'Amore*

Encore

Dr. Martin Luther King, Jr. Meets Verdi

If you think politics makes seemingly strange bedfel-

lows, get a load of classical music. It's not well known that Dr. Martin Luther King, Jr. was an opera buff. That's not as surprising as it may seem. His wife, Coretta Scott King, was a trained classical music singer during her years of study at the New England Conservatory of Music in Boston. One of her teachers was the noted Swedish-American soprano, Marie Sundelius. Sundelius performed in various stage productions at New York's Metropolitan Opera in the 1920s. One of those productions was Verdi's *Aida* in which she was the voice of a priestess.

Coretta at times waxed nostalgically about her love of classical music. As she put it in one interview: "In high school, I had a teacher who influenced me greatly. She exposed me to the world of classical music. Before then I had never heard classical music. She exposed me to the great composers of the world." In recognition of Dr. King's great love of classical music, the Atlanta Symphony often includes classical works in its various events that commemorate the life of Coretta and Martin. Who knows, even Verdi might well have nodded his approval at that.

Verdi didn't have one up on the French though. They weren't content with just good singing and a crisp drama. They went big—really big. In fact, they went grand, so grand that it quickly became known as the "Grand Opera." It uses every available technique: librettos, lots of ballets, stage machinery, choruses, and crowd scenes. The idea is to make opera a spectacle to please and delight crowds. There are long acts, a huge cast, a ballet, dramatic scenery, and remarkable lighting effects.

It was time to lighten things up on the stage, and the name they came up with gave that away: *Opera Comique.* Though not all those operas were laughers, those that were threw in lots of slapstick dialogue, pared back the singing, and skimped on the drama. They wanted it to be funny stuff that would tickle the audience's funny bones and leave them laughing in the aisles and still chuckling as they left the theater. Truly, it was entertainment for entertainment's sake.

It didn't take long for that light, escapist fare to draw the attention of crowds and a producer who was ever alert for a commercial opportunity. André Ernest Modeste Grétry (France,1741-1813) aimed to please in that regard. His most famous work was the historical "rescue opera," *Richard Coeur-de-lion* (1784), which achieved international popularity, reaching London in 1786 and later Boston, in 1797.

A couple of the more popular ones that took Paris by storm were written by a German, Giacomo Meyerbeer's (1791-1864) *Robert le Diable* (1831) and a few years later, his *Les Huguenots* (1836). I always thought it was odd that the French could eat up an opera written by a German.

Unlike the Italians, Germans, and French, the Brits never quite found their opera legs. There is really no defined school of English romantic opera. In fact, in some ways, it seems almost contradictory to use "English" and "opera" in the same sentence. Most people still pretty much think of opera as an Italian thing, and some credit the French, but a few

Brits did have some success with it. Henry Purcell (England, 1659-95) was the first, with his three-act *Dido and Aeneas* (1688?)

Decades later, John Barnett (England, 1802-90), a cousin of Meyerbeer's, composed a work in the romantic style of that period. Barnett mounted his opera, *The Mountain Sylph,* at the Lyceum Theatre in London in 1834, and it contained all the elements of romantic opera, including emphasis on elegant song styling and high drama. It went over quite well.

Sandwiched between these two was another Brit, John Gay (1685-1732), who used lots of spoken dialogue, folk songs, popular songs, and well-known arias in his *The Beggar's Opera* (1728). It was and still is the best-known example of the earlier English opera style. Gay had another distinction, one Handel couldn't have been too thrilled about. In fact, for a time, he almost put the great Handel out of business. Unlike Handel's pieces, Gay's opera was based on popular tunes. It was a lighthearted, talking and singing romp loved by the regular folks, and they flocked there in droves to see and hear it. Truly, it was a remarkable contrast to the overbearing, heavy-sledding religious stuff of the times, the opposite of Handel's operas and oratorios. As we all know, Handel eventually regained his legs as a big crowd-pleaser with *Messiah,* but it took time.

From My Concert Seat

I was always curious about what it took to knock Handel from the top spot on the opera perch for a time in England, so I listened to excerpts of Gay's opera on *YouTube.* I still don't get it, but that was England a long time ago.

Recommended Listening

J. Gay, *The Beggar's Opera, Introduction*

Encore

If at First You Don't Succeed

"I'm still completely devastated from everything that happened—not so much by what was done to my poor *'Butterfly,'* but with the poison directed toward me as an artist and a person. This premiere was an inferno a la Dante and was long in coming." So wrote Giacomo Puccini (Italy, 1858-1924). He was beyond crushed by the poor reception of his *Madama Butterfly* at its opening at Milan's Scala Opera House in February of 1904. The audience considered it such a stinker that they hooted with bird, cow, and goat calls. Still, the persistent Puccini didn't throw in the towel. He had worked hard on the opera, and he had faith in the story of a U.S. Marine officer

and a Japanese geisha, supposedly based on true events. He knew it deserved much, much better treatment than it got, so he tweaked it repeatedly and created a three-act production instead of the original two. He also shortened it in spots.

His efforts paid off, because when it reopened three months later, it was a smash, and hit has been a hit ever since. The moral of the story for composers is and always has been this: If you believe in your work and yourself, somewhere, sometime, an audience will believe in it too. Puccini was only the latest in a long line of composers who braved the initial boos and put-downs of their work, only to get the last laugh in the end. Not all composers would be so lucky.

* * * * *

I must come back to the point that opera, like classical symphonic music, has received a horrible rap. It is stereotyped as being only for those with upturned noses, the stuffed-shirt snobs, as if it cannot possibly resonate with any common folks living everyday lives. In reality, this is so far off the mark that a descriptive term has even been formulated to dispel that silly notion. *Verisimo,* meaning "true," derived from the Italian *vero,* took nineteenth-century opera by storm.

This type of opera presents everyday people, particularly lower class, real people, in real, everyday situations, often in situations and events that are trying, challenging, and sometimes brutal and sordid. The two operas most often cited as excellent examples of *verismo* are Pietro Mascagni's (Italy, 1755-1815) *Cavalleria Rusticana* and Ruggiero Leoncavallo's (Italy, 1857-1919) *I Pagliacci.* I've watched excerpts from the two on *YouTube,* and they both have a lot of gritty moments. Oftentimes, there is harshness in the singing, which is anything but the "beautiful voice" sound of the *bel canto.*

There is also the curious issue of whether opera really reflects the situations anyone ever really faces in life or whether the action is peculiar to the life experiences of the nation, be it France, Italy, Germany, or the U.S., whatever nation the composer hails from. This is really a straw man debate, for the answer is simply both.

Opera composers did a pretty good job of representing true life, especially of the lower classes in Italy and other countries. At the same time, they managed to include universal themes, relying on societal classes rather than nationalities. Every nation at every point in history has had its poor or working class. Opera can and often does portray tensions and conflicts between groups. For instance, Georges Bizet's (France, 1838-75) *Carmen* (1875) is one of the best-known, longest-enduring operas of all time. Why? In large part, the success of *Carmen* is because it depicts common folk, all the struggles of a working-class existence, tinged with a little immorality and lawlessness, as sex and violence are always good sellers. Spoiler alert here, but in my opinion, it was a good move for Bizet to knock off the main character in *Carmen,* a can't-miss formula for success. The opera is so universal in theme that anyone can read something into it, and that makes it relatable to all people.

Recommended Listening

Pietro Mascagni, *Cavalleria Rusticana, Intermezzo*

I can't leave things with opera here, for there is another applicable term: "word-drama." The man who did for opera what Beethoven did for the symphony, namely revolutionize it, avoided using the word "opera" to describe his works, which rank at the pinnacle of the opera genre. He flatly called his operas "drama with music words."

Richard Wagner (Germany, 1813-83) is as close to a household name among music lovers as one can get. I have fantasized many times about jumping on a plane and flying to the Bayreuth Festival in Germany to hear *The Flying Dutchman, Parsifal, Tannhauser, Lohengrin,* and, of course, his towering work, *Ring Cycle.* Even if I could, though, it would be a crap-shoot to get in; the concerts are so wildly popular that tickets are scarcer than the proverbial hen's teeth, and those concerts are sold out years in advance.

Wagner's works have dominated operatic stages everywhere, and an entire body of music literature and analysis exists on each one of them. His colorful life reads like an adventure novel; he was a scoundrel, philanderer, political rebel, fugitive, and notorious anti-Semite. Hitler's deification of him and his music has been well worked over, though, so I'll leave that alone.

From My Concert Seat

Wagner's life was so controversial that it was only natural for a bio-pic to be produced about him. The exhausting nine-hour marathon is a 1983 film series titled *Wagner.* It stars Englishman Richard Burton as the very German Wagner. I tried to watch it but gave up after three hours. It is a jumble, a mishmash that has the feel of a cut-and-paste, patchwork operation that does little to clarify or tell the Wagner story. Perhaps his life was just too Hollywood for Hollywood to even get a proper grasp on it.

Wagner is hailed as the big man in opera because he overwhelms the listener and viewer with massive, heart-stopping orchestral sound. He doubles down on the music by creating a gargantuan spectacle onstage. This is one reason his overtures are and always have been played as stand-alone concert pieces in and of themselves.

I'm always struck by the fact that when speaking about Wagner, critics never miss the chance to hammer the guy for being rotten, a man who shamelessly dogged friend and foe alike. He's always cited as the textbook example of a hated man whose music could still be beyond loved.

Recommended Listening

R. Wagner, *The Faust Overture*

Encore

Would Wagner Gag at or Applaud This?

In 1961, Wagner's grandson, Wieland Wagner, had a brainstorm. He decided to produce yet another production of Wagner's *Tannhaeuser* at Bayreuth. One of the divas that he invited to audition was the then 24 year old Grace Bumbry, an African-American. Now when some in the press got wind of this, the stuff hit the fan. They screamed that it was absolutely sacrilegious to even entertain the idea of a black singer, or as they put it, an *eine Schwarze,* in a Wagner opera.

Fortunately, the only voice that counted in the matter was Wieland's. He immediately cast her in the role ofVenus in the production. Bumbry made history by becoming the first person of color ever to be cast in a major role at the prestigious Bayreuth Festspielhaus. But more than that she gave a knockout performance in the role.

Now here's what's interesting. After her performance, the hitherto hostile press went nuts gushing over the *Die Schwarze* Venus." But even more interesting,. Wieland shrugged it all off and said the old man would

not have objected since he would want the best voice for the part, no matter her color.

Meanwhile two of the world's renowned operatic divas, Leotyne Price and Jessyne Norman, are African-American, and both have made huge marks in the opera world by singing Wagner. Price's rendition of the *"Liebestod"* from *Tristan und Isolde,* which she sang at the Ravinia Festival in 1985, still draws countless raves today. It is hailed by many as one of the best versions of the song ever recorded. Meanwhile, Norman has feasted on Wagner, singing and recording many of the favorites from Wagner's major operas. Twenty-two of them are on the *The Jessyne Norman Collection.*

Now, as I mentioned, Wagner has earned the much-deserved scurrilous reputation as a virulent anti-Semite and racial chauvinist of his day, but he was the supreme consummate artist too. Thus, the time capsule question is this: Since Norman and Price are equally supreme consummate artists, would Wagner have gagged at the thought of them singing his works, or would he have applauded them as tens of thousands of others have? This is yet another what-if scenario that I find quite intriguing, as there would be irony in either possible answer.

The symphony and opera are the 747s of classical music, the forms that pack 'em in at concert and opera halls and festivals. They make the reputations for the composers, conductors, and artists. They also pay the bills for a lot of composers.

Still, there are also the instrumental soloists and the smaller works they play. They may be the Piper Cubs of the concert hall, but they are just as important, captivating, and foundational in the evolution of classical music. In fact, they are often more edgy, bold, and cutting edge than the big-ticket stuff. I now turn to them and this form.

Clara Schumann

CHAPTER 8

A Guide to the Soloist

"You write to become immortal or because the piano happens to be open or you've looked into a pair of beautiful eyes."
—Robert Schumann

There really isn't much of a dispute that Bach, Handel, Mozart, and Beethoven are the unrivaled giants of instrumental classical music, but I can't stop with them. Several other names deserve to sit on the top shelf with them. My first introduction to one of them was the tune I heard many times, a melody that has danced into the ears of tens of thousands of brides, grooms, and wedding guests. That tune is the well-known *"Wedding March"* from *A Midsummer Night's Dream in E Major* (1826), written by seventeen-year-old Felix Mendelssohn (Germany, 1809-47), and he was off to the races with his career after he penned it.

Mendelssohn was a master at taking musical ideas from contemporaries and turning them into his own masterpieces of sound. His five symphonies, two piano concertos, and violin concerto feature gorgeous color, lots of expression, warmth, sublime beauty, power, flowing melodies, and even unpredictable rhythms. They set a high standard for composers, even those of his own time. When it came to style, he was a real throwback to Mozart. I mention him first in this chapter because he was such a brilliant piano soloist.

He and the other master soloists of that era not only extended the range of individual works, but they also shoved the solo performer to center stage. They mostly wrote for and played the piano, but their skill and virtuosity extended to the cello, violin, and oboe. These were the instruments they wowed and dazzled audiences with, nobility in particular. They often performed in exclusive recitals for the crowned heads of Europe, thus ensuring big paydays as well as much royal patronage and favoritism.

Mendelssohn brought the same sunburst beauty and power to his individual piano works. His *Seven Character Pieces and Songs Without Words,* (1829-45), for instance, prove that true virtuosity can be often be found simply in the playing of a piece.

From My Concert Seat

I'm a big symphony guy, and Mendelssohn is no exception. In fact, I am the proud owner of a boxed set of his five symphonies. His *Scottish* and *Italian* symphonies are among my favorite works. As for his small piano works, I've only listened to them a couple times on *YouTube.* While I must confess that they passed a bit over my

head and under my ear, what I did hear in them was a gentle, even dainty sound.

Encore

A Musician Who Was Literally an Artist

Mendelssohn was more than a first-rate composer; he was also a first-rate artist. I had the privilege of seeing some of his eye-catching watercolors on display in London during a visit in 1998. The vivid color, broad strokes, and naturalistic scenes were striking. His knack for painting served him well after the heartbreaking death of his musician-composer sister, Fanny, in 1847. Wielding the brush was therapeutic for him, and his series of watercolor landscapes were the product of his deep grief.

* * * * *

Whenever my mother was in one of her plaintive moods, she loved to sing or hum a song that I soon came to recognize. I didn't find out until much later that the song was *"Ave Maria,"* written by Franz Schubert (Germany, 1797-1828). He, like Mendelssohn, didn't live long; he only just crept over the proverbial hill and died at age thirty-one. As short as his life was, he packed a lot into it. His nine symphonies and hundreds of songs are a tour de force in the classical music tradition. His most important works, though, those for solo performance, are his eleven piano sonatas and *Wanderer Fantasy*

(1822) in four movements. What's really unique about it is that it's played without a break. The aim was to build, build, and build some more as the force of the piece drives toward a thunderous ending.

Franz Liszt, whom we'll meet in a moment, and other composers later adopted this form. Schubert, like Mendelssohn, will make a return engagement when I spotlight their symphonies.

Recommended Listening

F. Schubert, *Piano Sonatas D. 958, 959, and 960*

Schubert wrote hundreds of songs. He captured the lyrical beauty and sensuous ecstasy of song in his piano works. When I think about the smooth sound in singing, like that heard in modern groups like Manhattan Transfer, I think of Schubert.

There is really great curiosity about Schubert. Beyond the fact that he died at thirty-one, the other great pity is that much of his colossal output, including his quartets, masses, and symphonies, were not heard or even heard of during his lifetime. His *Symphony No. 9, "The Great"* (1840) is Beethoven-like in sweep, grandeur, and stature, but this last symphony of his didn't even turn up until years after his death. It is an interesting story, as two Englishmen, George Grove of *Grove's Dictionary* fame and Arthur Sullivan of Gilbert and Sullivan fame, took a trip to Vienna in 1867. There, they dug up five of his symphonies and dozens of his songs, as well as the incidental music to *Rosamunde* (1823), a play that didn't do much in its day. The elegant and lyrically lilting *Rosamunde,* though, is another story and has been played endlessly since its discovery.

The biggest Schubert find was his two-movement *Unfinished Symphony (Symphony No. 8)* in 1865, nearly forty years after his death. I love this story too. One of Schubert's so-called friends had squirreled it away, though no one really knows why. Despite endless speculation and theories throughout the years, no one will ever really know why Schubert didn't finish it. The work is tantalizing, slightly mysterious, and brooding, deeply personal in tone and sound.

It was inevitable that something with that name and sound would be snatched up by Hollywood. I first heard strains of it in the Peter Sellers 1979 dark comedy, *Being There,* and bits and pieces of it have been bandied around in several other films as well.

From My Concert Seat

I was hardly surprised that someone wouldn't be tempted to actually try to do what Schubert didn't and probably never intended to do by completing his *Unfinished Symphony.* For ages, prize-promising competitions have lured composers to take a crack at it, and many have tried. As the old biblical admonition goes, "many

are called, but few are chosen." In this case, even few is an overstatement, as no one has been truly successful at rewriting or modifying a Schubert work.

Encore

SCHUBERT'S ETERNAL BOND WITH BEETHOVEN

Schubert was a Vienna native during the same years while Beethoven lived there, but it isn't clear whether they actually met in life. Schubert was one of three composer pallbearers at Beethoven's funeral; he was so awestruck by Beethoven that as he lay on his deathbed at only thirty-one, one of his last requests was to hear Beethoven's *String Quartet No. 14,* and that request was granted. Schubert would not let death cheat him of getting close to Beethoven, and he even requested to be buried next to him. That request was also granted. In years to come, Schubert and Beethoven would have good company beside them when the waltz king family member, Johann Strauss II, and Brahms joined them. Their graves all lie side by side today.

Recommended Listening

F. Schubert, *Sonatas in A Minor, D. 537, B Major, D. 575,* and (at least in its original form) *E Flat Major, D. 568*

I don't immediately think of the names Schubert and Mendelssohn when I think of the premier solo pianists of their day. Rather, I think of Frederic Chopin (Poland, 1810-49). The sickly, expatriate from his native Poland to France and his decade long live-in relationship with novelist Amantine-Lucile-Aurore Dupin, popularly known as George Sand (France, 1804-76), has fascinated Chopin scholars for decades. His major big-ticket works are his two piano concertos, and there are no symphonies or operas on his résumé. He was a solo pianist's pianist. His twenty-seven *Etudes* and twenty-four *Preludes* and his *Nocturnes, Ballades, Mazurkas,* and *Waltzes* (all dance melodies) are standard teaching and learning pieces for piano students and teachers.

I have often heard these played as stand-alone pieces in concerts. His *Preludes* (1830s) are short and relatively light listening. Chopin is given lots of credit for giving the piano a free almost spontaneous sound.

To me, Chopin's twenty-four *Preludes* and concert *Etudes* and *Nocturnes* (1827-46) always sound loose and relaxed, with a lot of variety. He was also a rock-solid Polish patriot, and that feel and spirit of his native homeland comes through in his *Ballades* (1831-42).

Recommended Listening

F. Chopin, *Mazurka in B Minor Op. 33 No. 4* and *Piano Concert No. 1 in E Minor*

While Schubert and Mendelssohn aren't close to being my first options when I think of a piano great, this is even more the case with the tormented, tortured soul of classical music by Robert Schumann (Germany, 1810-56). His fits, depression, insanity, and, later, confinement to an institution and his ultimate death have been analyzed by classical music scholars from just about every imaginable angle, all of them trying to get a clue on his genius or torment. Schumann's four symphonies, cello concerto, and one grand-scale piano concerto, egged on by his wife Clara, whom I discussed previously, are genuine masterpieces of beauty and power.

Schumann composed a number of short character pieces for piano; even the titles stir the juices of a player, as well as the listener's imagination. One of his best-known major piano works, *Carnaval,* conjures up a picture of a masquerade ball. They are twenty short pieces in dance rhythm, named for a dance or costumed figure. Schumann liked the program idea so much that it crops up repeatedly in his piano works, and that makes for vivid listening.

So brilliant are his works that I can almost draw a mental picture of the musical images in his best-known ones for piano solo: *Pappillions* (1831), *Carnaval* (1834-35), and *Kinderszenen* (1838). He and Chopin weren't just playing notes. Instead, they were telling a story with and on the solo piano.

As a writer, I was especially interested in this note about Schumann. He was of that rare breed among musician-composers, a man who could write a first-rate, critical but objective view of music and musicians. He did so from 1834 to 1844 in the journal *Die Neue Zeischrift fur Musik (New Journal of Music),* which he founded and edited. He also used the journal to champion the music of Chopin, Brahms, and Schubert. He railed against what he believed was the empty virtuosity of some compositions and their composers and repeatedly called for a fuller, more robust expression of feeling and thought in the music.

From My Concert Seat

There is an ugly side note to this side note. When Schumann relinquished the editorship of his journal, the new editor published a piece by Wagner, a virulently anti-Semitic attack on Jewish composers and musicians. It was nineteenth-century Europe after all, and anti-Semitism came with the territory at the time. Jewish composers, from the classic world giants, like Mendelssohn and Mahler, as well as lesser ones, had to battle against this sort of thing all their lives. To escape the religious bigots, they became Catholics, Lutheran, or anything but Jewish. The conversions didn't help much, though, as both men still endured big and little slights throughout their lives about their birth religion, in spite of their musical prowess.

Recommended Listening

R. Schumann, *Carnaval, Op. 9*

Encore

Ever Wonder Why Orchestras Tune Up?

Schumann took a stab at conducting, but he wasn't very successful. Mendelssohn, on the other hand, was hailed as one of the truly great conductors of the day during his stint as conductor of one of Europe's greatest orchestras then and now, the Leipzig Gewandhaus Orchestra. Both men had to deal with one aspect of the orchestra that concert-goers are familiar with: the tune-up. The concertmaster strides to the stage before the conductor and plays a tuning note for the rest of the musicians to match. The tuning instrument is really the oboe, in the note of A. The idea is to make sure all the instruments are totally in sync and playing on key.

Some claim this is done just for show, mostly to please the expectant audience, since the orchestra should already have tuned up before they hit the stage. Others say it's absolutely necessary to tune onstage to make sure everyone is hitting the right key. Regardless, tradition is tradition, and it will likely continue, no matter the reason.

* * * * *

I have seen so many great virtuoso pianists in concerts that I've lost count. They all have their own way of doing things onstage, yet they share one commonality: They know all eyes in the audience are glued on them, and they are the show. They can thank one composer for making stage presence as much a part of a solo performance as the playing itself. Franz Liszt (Germany, 1811-86) pioneered the piano recital, along with that of other instruments. He brought audacious, showy, and dazzling virtuosity to his piano performances, complete with hair flying, arms waving, and head rocking back and forth before head-banging was cool. Many pianists, in one way or another, try to emulate some or all of that in their performances.

Musicologists love to label Liszt as the first true rock star, especially since women mobbed the stage to touch and ogle him while he played it for all it was worth. Hans Christian Anderson—yes, the famed fabler himself—attended one of his concerts in 1840 and was thoroughly awed by him. Said the storyteller: "The instrument appeared to be changed into a whole orchestra, and when he finished playing, the flowers rained down on him." I'll talk more about Liszt when I discuss tone poems.

For now, though, in discussing soloists, we shall regard his Three Concert Etudes (1845-49), typical of his virtuosic technique. The sound is exciting and dynamic. A number of his piano works are transcriptions of other composer's songs and symphonies and operatic paraphrases of songs on popular opera. This was not uncommon. Great composers then and now have always been fascinated with the works of other composers. If the material from another sounds good and plays well, they see no problem with transcribing it and using it in another musical form.

From My Concert Seat

I've often noted that a pianist will sometimes close their eyes and talk to the keys while lovingly caressing them. I watched noted Russian pianist Olga Korn do this while playing the elegant second movement of Edvard Grieg's *Piano Concerto in A Minor* (1858) at a concert of the New Mexico Philharmonic in April of 2015. It was a pure, sensual connect between an artist and her instrument, and there was something beautiful about it that really came through in the music.

Encore

LISZT: THE FIRST ROCK STAR?

"Liszt deliberately placed the piano in profile to the audience so they could see his face. He'd whip his head around while he played, his long hair flying, beads of sweat shooting into the crowd. He was the first performer to stride out from the wings of the concert hall to take his seat at the piano. Everything we recognize about the

modern piano recital—think Keith Jarrett, Glenn Gould, Tori Amos or Elton John—Liszt did first. Even the name 'recital' was his invention."

Recommended Listening

F. Liszt, *Etude in D Flat Major*

* * * * *

I can't possibly leave this discussion of the soloist and the smaller forms without a brief nod to Bach, Mozart, and Beethoven. Bach's *Goldberg Variations* (1741) and *Well-Tempered Clavier,* I mentioned before. Since he played the harpsichord for them, it was only natural that he spotlight the harpsichord. He accomplished this by making the notes sparkle in all keys, with lots of variety, offering up a very unique sound that has made great listening for three centuries.

Mozart's style is a little different. He lets the musical themes unfold naturally and spontaneously. His notes are measured and often extended to achieve maximum listening effect. He is also great at conveying feeling and much variety in the piano sound. He was one of the world's best natural opera composers, if not the world's best. It's fitting, then, that many of his piano works are song-like. The *Piano Sonata in F* and *Piano Concerto in E* (1785) are two good examples. I've heard them both many times, and I could actually see the song-like quality in them rather than simply hearing it. That, in and of itself, says a lot; only a great composer lets listeners see his or her music.

Beethoven went further and used powerful contrasts to broaden the expressive range of the piano. Forget tickling the ivories; he pounded them! Just as his *Seventh Symphony* set me off on my journey of discovery on the classical music road, Beethoven's *Piano Concerto No. 5, "The Emperor"* (1809-11), his last, has always been a close second, in my opinion. That particular piece is a big, bold, expansive work that captures the passion and verve of the mature Beethoven. There is the grand entrance opening, the dreamy Mozart-like second movement, and the blazing finish. It never fails to alternately stir joy and sentimentality in me. One night, a friend of mine literally swooned during the playing of the second movement of *"The Emperor"* concerto at a summer concert at the Hollywood Bowl. It has that effect.

An interesting side note on its nickname, *"The Emperor"*: Like most of the nicknames of a grand, new piece by a major composer, this was not Beethoven's doing. His English publisher, Johann Baptist Cramer, sniffed more dollars in having a catchy nickname befitting its grandeur, rather than simply calling it *Piano Concerto No. 5.*

The piano or violin are not the only instruments for which solos have been written. In fact, the most widely used solo instrument of all will always be the human voice. I think the consensus among most musicologists is that Schubert is, perhaps, the leader when it comes to writing for this particular instrument. He wrote over 600 *Lieder* or songs based on poems. His songs are intensely elegiac, dripping with passion. There is much contrast and change within them, depicted by repeating and varying the notes and melody. Schubert's song melodies are pure beauty, like rhythmic poetry in motion. This brings me back to Schubert's big, perennial tear-jerker, "*Ave Maria.*" If I think of a celestial song, this is the one.

Schumann was no slouch either when it came to first-class song-writing, as he penned over 120 of them. Like Schubert, he saw song as poetry, with the voice and piano as equal partners. His *Lovely Month of May* (1840) is based on a poem. In it, he gives the piano an equal role as the voice to fully express a particular emotion in the song-poem. His *A Poets Love, A Woman's Love of Lif*e (1840) virtually drips with tearful sentimentalism.

Recommended Listening

F. Schubert, *Ave Maria*

Schubert and Schumann moved the dial higher and higher for other composers bent on song-writing. There were a number of them in the nineteenth century. Gabriel Faure (France, 1845-1924) wrote many songs, including *Cing Melodies de Venise and la Bonne Hanson* (1891). Hector Berlioz (France, 1803-69) wrote the song cycle, *Les Nuits d'ete* (1841). Charles Gounod (France, 1818-93) wrote many songs or melodies, and the popular *Maid of Athens* (1872) is one example. These are all beautiful, poetic works in song.

Understandably, they were unabashedly popular songs geared to a popular audience. The critics soon picked up on this and began referring to them as "art songs." Even Beethoven couldn't resist writing a few of them. He penned a few, a set of six, in a song cycle that named *An Die Ferne Geliebte* (1816) (i.e., a circle or ring of song). He expresses all kinds of moods, in different keys: joy, sorrow, pleasure, pain, and more. According to *The Music History Guide,* Beethoven called them the *Liederkreis an Die Ferne Geliebte.* The songs are written so that the theme of the first song reappears as the conclusion of the last, forming a song circle *(Liederkreis),* a ring in the figurative sense of a finger-ring as a love token rather than a song cycle *(Liederzyklus),* in the sense of a program or drama.

From My Concert Seat

As for another what-if, since I never really associated Beethoven with song-writing, I have to wonder what would have happened if he had really put his mind to it. Could he have been a great songwriter too? If that happened, would some of those songs eventually find their way into a pop, rock, or even R&B songwriter's playbook. Actually, now that I think of it, the second movement of Beethoven's *Pathetique Sonata* was used by Billy Joel as the chorus of his tune, *"This Night."* It was in limited re-

lease and didn't make anyone's top ten, but the thought of a top-ten Beethoven pop song somewhere is tantalizing nonetheless. By the way, Joel gave Beethoven credit as one of the songwriters.

If there is any one timeframe in the history of classical music that can be called the golden age, it was the nineteenth century. There was Beethoven, Schubert, Mendelssohn, and Wagner, as well as many other figures who shaped and defined that age and wildly pushed the limits of technique, form, and even the sound of classical music outward as well as inward, to new and exciting directions. It's time to meet them.

Gustav Mahler

CHAPTER 9

A Guide to the Romantics

The echo of Beethoven's Ninth Symphony's "Ode to Joy" in the grand melody of the Johannes Brahms Symphony No. 1 finale is particularly obvious: When a critic called the similarity to Brahms's attention, his testy reply was, "Any ass can see that!"

—Johannes Brahms

I would have loved to see the look on the face of the know-it-all critic who implied that Brahms stole from Beethoven for the last movement of his first-ever symphony, but it was really an insult and an accusation Brahms faced constantly—one he often bristled at. Then again, classical music would not be classical music at all without its raging debates over what is fit to be called original or even authentic classical music. This was especially true in the period of the nineteenth century known as the Romantic Era. Wagner ignited some of the fiercest debates among German and other late nineteenth-century composers, a debate that continues to this day. For some, there was no in-between: One either loved or hated the guy.

Johannes Brahms (Germany, 1833-97) was on one side. He represented the old-school throwback to Mozart and Beethoven, and he was the keeper of the so-called "pure" classical style, form, and sound. There wasn't much deviation from that rigid structure in his four symphonies. By any stretch, this does not suggest that his symphonies lack color, range, passion, and intense feeling in any way. It's no accident that Brahms has settled comfortably in as the third B (Bach, Beethoven, Brahms) in the pantheon of classical music composers. He was fussy, meticulous, and a near perfectionist when it came to composing. Like his counterparts, he simply had to get it right.

For a decade before he premiered *Symphony No. 1,* his desire for perfection caused him to carry around the rambunctious, brash, and even monumental piece, with its forty-plus, pounding drum beat opening. It was not released until 1876. Brahms supposedly took so much time with it because he was terrified of being compared to Beethoven, only to fall short of those lofty expectations. He moved much faster with his softer, gentler, and much mellower *Symphony No. 2* (1877) and brought it out only a little more than a year after the first. His piano concertos are impassioned, grand, and filled with alternately stormy and sublime sounds. Likewise, his *Piano Concerto No. 1* (1858) is similar, said to be a gentle, moving nod to his good friend and champion, Schumann, who had passed by then.

Opera wasn't for him though. He briefly considered taking a shot at writing one but backed off in the end. Thus, the world would have to make due with his *Academic Festival Overture,* which was written in the summer of 1880 as a so-called musical thank-you, of sorts, to the University of Breslau, which had awarded him an honorary doctorate in 1879. Hopefully, the stuffy academics there had a sense of humor, because the Overture is a lighthearted, jolly work that Brahms stuffed with rousing, tavern, and student drinking songs. His *The Tragic Overture* (1880) is aptly named.

From My Concert Seat

It had been years since I'd heard *The Tragic Overture* played in concert, so I was disappointed when leading Estonian Conductor Neeme Jarvi programmed it with the L.A. Philharmonic in April of 2015 and I had to miss the performance because of my flight delay from a concert in Albuquerque. Truly, it was tragic for me!

As one might ascertain from their names, *The Tragic Overture* is the diametric opposite of the Festival Overture in its somber, turbulent, almost tortured sound. Since there is no opera in Brahm's playbook, his *German Requiem* (1865-68) fits the bill for a big composition for instruments and choir. His *Violin Concert in D Major* (1878) is almost always lumped together with Beethoven, Mendelssohn, and Tchaikovsky's violin concertos as the unsurpassed works for violin and orchestra of any composer of all time. I've heard them played so often by major and small orchestras that I almost feel I could play them myself, even though I can't play a note on any instrument.

Recommended Listening

J. Brahms, *Violin Concerto in D Major*

The mid to late nineteenth century was a time when composers seemingly had to take sides: They could either conform to the old ways of writing and composing or jump onboard with the stylistic revolution in sound that Wagner had brought in with his freewheeling, powerhouse operas. Brahms was on one side, while Liszt Anton Bruckner (Austria, 1824-96); Gustav Mahler (Germany, 1860-1911), at least to an extent; and Richard Strauss (Germany, 1864-1949) were on the other. They all found ways to accommodate their mostly orchestral and symphonic tone poems to Wagner's style and approach.

Liszt, however, really struck out on his own, as he was determined to use music to tell a story. That was a huge departure from the formal structure of the symphony. I'll discuss him and the tone poem in more detail in a moment.

Before that, let us consider the deeply religious Bruckner. He infused his sacred masses and, most importantly, his nine symphonies into a reverent, liturgical approach that came through in the tone and sound. The Wagnerian influence was plainly heard in the massive structure of his symphonies; for instance, his last one, *Symphony No. 9*, was unfinished and stitched together from what he had managed to pull together at the time of his death in 1896. An hour-plus in length, this patchwork of music is packed with flowing harmonies, and he repeats whole passages. Despite the mind-numbing length of his symphonies and the mocking slur that he wrote the same symphony nine times, Bruckner has found a big renaissance in the concert halls the last couple decades.

As is the case with many pieces of music, this one has a most interesting back-story. The dying Bruckner nightly beseeched God, quite like Haydn did, to give him the strength to finish the symphony. "If He refuses, then He must take responsibility for its incompleteness," he decided. Since his prayer wasn't answered, others took the liberty to try to finish the work for him after his death, but perhaps Bruckner was on to something in saying it was best left to God's hands, for all who attempted to finish it only botched it badly. In the 1930s, though, researchers took a close look at his original notes and matched it with his score, then reordered the symphony in full alignment with Bruckner's style.

From My Concert Seat

I've heard Bruckner's *Ninth* in concert a number of times. With each rendition I am not sure if what I'm hearing is what Bruckner wrote or intended or if it is merely that someone else didn't take the time to make sure it

was just that. If anything proves the old "Time heals all wounds" adage, the case of Bruckner certainly does.

Recommended Listening

A Bruckner, *Symphony No. 4 in E Flat Major, "Romantic"*

Bruckner was hardly the only long-winded Romantic Era composer who was, more or less, influenced by Wagner. Mahler can stretch out material and time with the best of them. His nine symphonies are long, with the same vibrant harmonies, emotion, and drama. Some even have a program description. His *Symphony No. 6, "Tragic"* (1903-04), for instance, seems to depict defeat and death in the end. He was obsessively preoccupied with that in his life, and it inevitably seeped through in his music. The vague spiritualism, akin to a biblical theme, can be heard in his *Symphony No. 2, "The Resurrection"* (1888-94), one of my favorites. It is large, wide-ranging, tumultuous, and all over the musical map, with its theme of death, salvation, and judgment day. The choral ending in the closing movement lifts to a crescendo and conveys a musical word picture of the eternal joy of resurrection.

From My Concert Seat

I was so moved by Sir Simon Rattle's recording of the *Resurrection* symphony that I called his publicist af-

ter a performance I saw at Disney Hall in 2012 with the L.A. Philharmonic Orchestra. I had to thank him for the superb recording, and he was quite gracious about it.

Mahler also didn't take any chances. To prevent some know-it-all critic from mistaking what he was trying to say with his music, he wrote detailed programs for his first four symphonies. He later had a second thought about trying to describe his symphonies and said the music should speak for itself; however, what he said about it when he wrote the programs for the four symphonies was in line with what a tone poem is all about. It was a big break from the past, in that it allowed composers the freedom to roam in a work without being bound by the stiflingly set form of the four-movement symphony. The added plus with the new musical form was that the composers could tell a yarn or borrow from a good one in life or literature and carry that to their music.

Encore

Poetic Justice

Mahler experienced one of the more fascinating odysseys in classical music. His music has been in, out, in, out, and in again at different points after his death in 1911. A few big-name conductors, such as Leopold Stokowski, championed his music and tried to revive interest in it, but the performances of his music during the 1920s

and 1930s were spotty at best except—ironically—in Germany and Austria.

I say "ironically" because Mahler was Jewish. As we all know, Hitler would have moved Heaven and Earth to expunge anything that had even the faintest hint of Jewish involvement with it, be it composer or musician, from the concert stage. Nevertheless, just before Mahler's music was officially banned as "degenerate," it was often played in German and Austrian concert halls between 1934 and 1938. To the shock of many, Mahler's music was performed at Berlin concerts by Jewish orchestras and for Jewish audiences only, as late as 1941, as well as in Amsterdam during the German occupation of the Netherlands. Not for a moment was there any doubt that the great music of such a great composer would survive the naysayers, and Mahler's, in a way, even defeated the cruel Hitler. That is truly pure poetic justice.

Recommended Listening

G. Mahler, *Adagietto, Symphony No. 5 in C Sharp Minor*

In their wildest dreams, neither Haydn nor Mozart likely envisioned a time when any composer would boldly announce that he was going to tell a story with his work and that it would be important enough to compete with the symphony, but the tone poem did just that in the mid-nineteenth century. As the name suggests, the tone poem conveys a particular mood, feeling, and the impression of any- and everything: a nature scene, a personality, an event, a happening, a play, or a drama. The composers spelled out their exact intent in the tone poem, all in one movement; as noted, it does not have the formal structure of a symphonic work, which generally consists of four movements.

Beethoven kinda-sorta kicked things off with his *Symphony No. 6, "The Pastoral"* (1808), his homage to nature: trees, bird sounds, and weather, such as the storm and clearing. At the end, there is a prayer off thanks for the awesome beauty and power of nature. The instruments played a specific role in this type of work, and that was to express the mood of each depicted scene. The woodwinds and strings are the sound of calm and serenity. The timpani (drums) and trombones are the sound of the thunder of the coming storm.

I must give Mendelssohn some credit for providing a strong hint about where a programmed symphony could go with his breezy, sunny, color-drenched, *Symphony No. 4, "The Italian."* As the name suggests, it was inspired by his jaunt to Italy in 1831, and much of it drips with all the festive cheer of an Italian festival. He said as much in a letter to his sister, Fanny, from Rome: "It will be the jolliest piece I have ever done." The last movement, the finale, clearly carries the moving melody of the Italian dance, the *tarantella.*

From My Concert Seat

In one stretch of time, over the course of one year, I heard Mendelssohn's other arguable program symphony, *Symphony No. 3, "The Scottish"* played, back to back, by orchestras at concerts in Santa Barbara and Culver City, California. After that, I was even more baffled as to why he insisted that he never regarded this symphony or his *Hebrides Overture* (1830) as having anything remotely to do with Scotland, when it clearly did.

Mendelssohn actually got the inspiration for his symphony from a visit to Scotland in 1829, but it would take him thirteen years to finally finish it, in 1842. He later admitted that some of the feeling and mood he got from the trip eased into the work. As he put it, "It is in pictures, ruins, and natural surroundings that I find the most music."

He may have been reluctant to call his work a program work, but I'd have to argue with him on that. Hector Berlioz (France, 1803-69) would likely take my side, as his *Symphonie Fantastique* (1830) is the complete package in a program symphony work. It includes love, the dance, foreboding, death, the march to the scaffold, and his longing for a woman, Harriet Smithson. *Symphonie Fantastique* has probably been written about, dissected and re-dissected, interpreted and reinterpreted, analyzed and reanalyzed almost as much as any of Mozart's or Beethoven's most popular major works.

Hollywood even took notice of "*The Dream of a Witches' Sabbath*," the part used as the haunting, macabre music in the 1991 Julia Roberts hit, *Sleeping with the Enemy.*

It's actually the fifth movement in the work. Berlioz pulls out all stops with its grotesque spirits, monsters, sorcerers, groans, yells, screams, and cries. The witches whirl around in an orgy of revelry and, ultimately, death. The bells, gongs, chimes, and drums tell the macabre part of this tale in music. This is heady stuff for a composer who only wrote one symphony. The piece is so out of the box that no matter how many times I hear it in concert, it always sounds fresh, with a tinge of spooky foreboding.

Recommended Listening

H. Berlioz, *Harold in Italy, Op. 16 - I. Harold in the Mountains (Part 1)*

From My Concert Seat

I vividly remember the monkey tossing the bone up in the air in the opening scene of Stanley Kubrick's 1968 film, *2001: A Space Odyssey.* I remember the slow melody that builds to a crashing fanfare in that scene, and it is the loud opening to *Thus Sprach Zarathustra* (1896), based on German Philosopher Friedrich Wilhelm Nietzsche's prose poem that explored the idea of a superman who stands

above the Christian and spiritual concept of good and evil. I occasionally use this to jolt my listening audience when I start one of my radio shows, for it even jolts me!

Liszt may have been the natural father of the tone poem, but the name most often thought of today when tone poems are played is the one who practically made a living off of writing them, Richard Strauss (Germany, 1864-1949). He wrote a string of them: *Ein Heldenleben, Don Juan* (1888), *Don Quixote* (1897), *Death and Transfiguration* (1888), and *Till Eulenspiegel* (1894-95). All of these are played endlessly on concert bills, and I've heard them often. They are big, bombastic, splashy works rich in harmony and color, producing a grandiose sound. They are based on literary works such as Cervantes's *Don Quixote.* Strauss wasn't content in just recycling a story for his tone poem. He went one better, though he sometimes shied away from claiming this. He saw himself as the hero of the work, and he was all of age thirty-four when he wrote it. This is exactly what his sweeping, blustery, heavy-on-the-horns *Ein Heldenleben* (1898) literally translates to: "*A Hero's Life!*"

Encore

SHOULD ART TRUMP POLITICS?

"To Richard Strauss, the composer, I take off my hat," Conductor Arturo Toscanini once famously declared. "To Richard Strauss, the man, I put it on again." Toscanini pos-

es the ancient dilemma: Should art trump politics?

Strauss thrived under Hitler. He was president of Hitler's *Reichsmusikkammer* (Reich Music Chamber), even while privately professing abhorrence of Nazi politics and Hitler's racist, murderous philosophy. Strauss was later mostly exonerated by the de-Nazification courts in Germany after World War II for aiding and abetting Hitler's regime. Still, in effect, his presence cosigned Hitler's grotesque crimes. Does that detract from the greatness of his art? Toscanini's quip about Strauss stands as the best answer to this eternal dilemma of what one is to make of a great artist who does horrid things or is complicit in the face of them. We must celebrate their art, even if we cannot celebrate the artist.

Strauss must not have the last word on the tone poem, so we'll look at Liszt a bit more. His *Prometheus* (1850, 1855), *Mazeppa* (1851), and *Orpheus* (1853-54) are based, respectively, on poems and an opera. His most popular work, *Les Preludes,* is based on a poem by nineteenth-century French Poet Alphone de Lamartine, *Nouvelles Méditations Poétiques* (1823). It is a great example of Liszt's method of providing unity, variety, and narrative to a work to tell a story in the work. The notes are written specifically to take on the different characters in the story. This makes *Les Preludes* (1854) and other tone poems stand out as something new, invigorating, and distinctive.

From My Concert Seat

Like me, I'm sure others still remember ol' Flash Gordon fighting off the bad guys in the series of the 1930s, which was often looped on TV in the 1950s. What you may not realize is that Flash fought it out with them to the thundering tones of *Les Preludes.*

The tone poem was not strictly a German or central European affair, for French composers also had a hand in writing them. One was a transplanted Belgian, a master organist and teacher, Cesar Franck (1822-92). *His Le Chasseur Maudit (The Accursed Huntsman)* (1882) is one of the most enchanting, beguiling pieces, incorporating superbly creative use of the form.

This piece was inspired by the ballad *Der Wilde Jäger (The Wild Hunter)* by German Poet Gottfried August Bürger. In it, Franck tells the story of a count who dares to go hunting on a Sunday morning, in violation of the Sabbath. The notes, orchestration, and instruments eerily capture the count's hunting horn, the church bells, the sacred chants, and the fearsome voice that condemns him to be pursued by evil spirits for eternity as payment for his transgression. You don't have to be a horror buff to hear that the dark, ominous mode of the music literally tells the tale. The youngsters at the University of Southern California's Thornton Symphony Orchestra played it in 2013, and it was one of the best performances I have heard of this piece; they expertly nailed the creepy sound of the work.

* * * * *

The English weren't big on tone poems; however, they reached back in time and grabbed material from their old folk and religious songs, then wrapped some pieces around them. Ralph Vaughn Williams reached back to the sixteenth century for a traditional English hymn written by a then-popular religious and court composer Thomas Tallis and spun off *Fantasia on a Theme of Thomas Tallis* (1910). It hit the big screen as featured music in the 2003 film, *Master and Commander: The Far Side of the World,* starring Russell Crowe. Williams followed this with the romantic, memorable, and very popular work, *Fantasia on Greensleeves* (1929). Again, Hollywood came calling, and they have often used this number, in one form or another, in films with syrupy romantic themes.

Recommended Listening

C. Franck, *Le Chasseur Maudit (The Accursed Huntsman)*

Williams's good friend and countryman, Gustav Holst, went a little further. In fact, he went far out into the galaxy and astrology. A big student of Indian mythology and astrological signs, Holst (England, 1874-1934) took a lot of years to compose a piece that aligned the galaxy with what became his masterwork over time, aptly named *The Planets* (1914-16). It has a big-bang opening with pounding, pulsating, hard-driving drums, cymbals, and horns that represent Mars, the old Roman god of war. Holst gives each of the planets in the piece a musical character that matches their astrological sign: peace, calm, tranquility, mirth, pathos, energy, fun, mischievousness, and so on.

From My Concert Seat

I heard *The Planets* played three times by three different orchestras in January and February of 2015, but the one that got the most creative with it was the New West Symphony Orchestra, enhancing their performance with a pictorial display of the planets on a big screen above the stage. It was imaginative, yes, but in all honesty, it didn't make me feel as if I was about to embark on an interplanetary excursion. The music was enough for me.

Benjamin Britten (England, 1913-76) stayed much closer to Earth and found the perfect setting for a musical tale on the theme of intolerance, violence, and death in the mid-nineteenth-century tale of a fisherman, Peter Grimes. The opera he based the tale on has done well over the years, but what has done far better for Britten is the *Four Sea Interludes* Op. 33, the instrumental music from *Peter Grimes* (1945). It depicts the harsh, foreboding, forbidding land and seascape and the tragic drama that engulfs Grimes. I actually heard this played, back to back, by two different orchestras at two different concerts in early 2015. Both captured the chill and the grim feel that Britten conveyed in the work of the desolate English seacoast town two centuries ago.

The English were ever creative when it came to dredging up new ways to tell a story with music. Sir Edward Elgar (England, 1857-1934) hit upon the idea of telling a story not based on an old story but on that of living people, namely his friends and associates. To sweeten the deal, he kept the world endlessly speculating and trying to guess who he was talking about. He did just that in his *Variations* Op. 36, better known as *The Enigma Variations* (1898-99), which has kept musicologists in a tizzy since its original unveiling. Each of the sections of the work carries the initials of the subject of description of people he knew. He describes their foibles and strengths, likes and dislikes, temperament and personal character as he saw them, and he accomplishes this with the full range of lyricism, wit, force, sarcasm, melancholy, and sublimity. I wonder just what Elgar's friends thought of his characterization of them, especially the less flattering ones. We'll never know, and it's probably just as well.

Recommended Listening

E. Elgar, *The Enigma Variations, Op. 36*

Encore

WHAT A TONE POEM SAYS

The text preface to Liszt's 1856 published score of *Les Preludes* explains exactly what he had in mind with this tone poem and what the music expressed:

"What else is our life but a series of preludes to that unknown Hymn, the first and solemn note of which is intoned by Death? Love is the glowing dawn of all existence; but what is the fate where the first delights of happiness are not interrupted by some storm, the mortal blast of which dissipates its fine illusions, the fatal lightning of which consumes its altar; and where is the cruelly wounded soul which, on issuing from one of these tempests, does not endeavor to rest his recollection in the calm serenity of life in the fields? Nevertheless, man hardly gives himself up for long to the enjoyment of the beneficent stillness which at first he has shared in Nature's bosom, and when 'the trumpet sounds the alarm,' he hastens, to the dangerous post, whatever the war may be, which calls him to its ranks, in order at last to recover in the combat full consciousness of himself and entire possession of his energy."

Old-time critics tore into this. In their eyes and ears, the tone poem horribly defiled musical tradition. One of the best-known critics of that day, Eduard Hanslick, led the charge.

After hearing a performance of *Les Preludes* in 1857, he flatly declared it heresy to try to tell a story with music, but in spite of his opinion, the tone poem had arrived and was here to stay.

Surely, Liszt or Strauss shouldn't have the last word on writing musical pictures of things, for a slew of other noted composers of that time were also tone poem practitioners. They added yet another element to it, namely their country. Edvard Grieg (Norway, 1843-1907), with his *Peer Gynt* (1875), and Bedrick Smetana (Czechoslovakia, 1824-84) with his *The Moldau* (1874), taken from the song cycle *Ma Vlast (My Fatherland),* the country's major river, conveyed the deep sense of national feeling in their music. They drew heavily on and were inspired by the dances, the folk tales, the songs, the myths, legends, and the natural settings of their respective countries. However, leave it to the Russians and a couple Hungarians to take nationalism and painting musical pictures about Russian and Hungarian culture and life to the extreme.

Recommended Listening

B. Smetna, *"The Moldau" (from Ma Vlast)*

I've always considered "the mighty handful," the name the five Russian composers were tagged with, is somewhat pretentious, since many of them then and now are hardly household names among classical music buffs. Undeniably, though, they did create a very distinct Russian sound in their music that incorporated the sounds of village songs, peasant dance music, Russian Orthodox Church chants, and folk tunes in their works. They are tuneful, dance-like, and extremely colorful pieces. The Russians may have written them for Russians, but they are delightful and timeless listening for anyone.

Here's a checklist of their names, but take special note of the titles of their best-known works for a tip on how they tried to capture the spirit of Russian culture and life: Alexander Borodin's (1833-87) *On the Steps of Central Asia;* Nikolai Rimsky-Korsakov's (1844-1908) *A Life for the Tsar;* Modest Mussorgsky's (1839-1881) opera, *Boris Godunov* (1868-73); Cesar Cui's (1835-1918) *Feast in a Time of Plague;* and Mily Balakirev's (1837-1910) *Islamey* and *Tamara.*

From My Concert Seat

Mussorgsky's *Pictures at an Exhibition* (1873) deserves a special mention here. It was originally a set of piano pieces that Maurice Ravel orchestrated. I've heard it often in concert. Its booming, banging, thunderous, closing movement tribute to Kiev's great medieval gates, "The Great Gate of Kiev," is a great concert closer. It always brings the entire audience to our feet, no matter what orchestra is playing it.

I've probably heard the composer who was not one of those five in concert almost as much as I've hear Beethoven. Peter Ilyich Tchaikovsky (1840-93) is much closer to being an old-school classic symphony guy. His six numbered symphonies did not stray from the standard four-movement model and symphonic form. He did, however, borrow heavily from traditional Russian folk themes and embed them in his symphonies. The best example of that is his *Symphony No. 2, "The Little Russian"* (1872), which is virtually a musical tribute to Ukrainian folk music; at the time, The Ukraine was known as "Little Russia," and judging from the warfare with Mother Russia that is currently raging, many in Big Russia still want to make it Little Russia again.

When asked to pay tribute to the czar and country with a musical number, Tchaikovsky did his patriotic duty, like all Russian composers in nineteenth-century Russia. In 1880, when he was asked to write a suitable but rousing patriotic number to commemorate Russia's trounce of Napoleon in 1812, he dutifully complied. He was never personally a huge fan of it, but *The War of 1812 Overture* has become the go-to piece when flags are waved and definitely not only in Russia. In fact, a lot of Independence Day celebrations in the good ol' U.S. of A. wouldn't be complete without noise, fireworks, and his overture.

Indeed, Tchaikovsky's prodigious output of symphonies, piano and violin concertos, ballets, and innumerable small chamber works include a lot of Russian folk music and Russian life; however, that's less important than the fact that he is second to none among the old masters when it comes to sheer, raw, almost animalistic power, energy, and passion in his music. To me, he is the king of the big, explosive sound in a symphonic work. Whether that had anything to do with his agonizing personal and sexual torment over his disguised homosexuality (it was the nineteenth century after all), I don't really know. Then again, no one really does. What I know is that when I hear a Tchaikovsky symphony, I know it.

Recommended Listening

P.I. Tchaikovsky, *Symphony No. 2 C Minor, "Little Russian"*

Encore

ONE GREAT PIANIST'S LOSS

This story is often told, mostly because Tchaikovsky told it about the initial rejection of his all-time renowned *Piano Concerto No. 1* by composer and piano great Nikolai Rubinstein (Russia, 1835-81). Though Tchaikovsky didn't dedicate the work to him as wrongly thought, he badly wanted him to perform the work at one of the 1875 concerts of the Russian Musical Society in Moscow. As the story goes, Rubinstein declined, supposedly calling it "unplayable."

Three years later, in a letter to Rubinstein, Tchaikovsky told his side of the story, his version of what hap-

pened when he played it: "I played the first movement. Not a single word, not a single remark! I fortified myself with patience and played through to the end. Still silence. I stood up and asked, 'Well?' Then a torrent poured from Nikolay's mouth, gentle at first, then more and more, growing into the sound of a Jupiter Tonana. It turned out that my concerto was worthless and unplayable; passages were so fragmented, so clumsy, so badly written that they were beyond rescue; the work itself was bad, vulgar; in places, I had stolen from other composers; only two or three pages were worth preserving; the rest must be thrown away or completely rewritten."

Rubinstein partly softened and said that if Tchaikovsky radically revised it, he'd consider playing it. For the countless number of composers whose works that. in time. would be hailed as masterpieces in sound but were initially called garbage, Tchaikovsky's retort to him stands for the ages: "'I shall not alter a single note,' I answered. 'I shall publish the work exactly as it is!' This I did."

Recommended Listening

P.I. Tchaikovsky, *Violin Concerto in D Major*

I must add that Tchaikovsky did not really dig his heels in the sand as he suggested in this letter. It was undoubtedly a great concerto, but even a great work can be made even greater with a little tinkering, so he did budge a bit and spruced it up in a few spots. A slightly revised version hit the concert stage in 1879 and even another one a decade later. What got off to a bad start with Rubinstein finished with a happy ending. In the end, not only did he rave about the work, but he also played it a number of times, just as countless others have done since.

It seemed poor Tchaikovsky didn't have much initial luck with his great works, though, for an almost identical fate befell his *Violin Concerto in D Major* (1878). Many critics were savage in their reviews, and a couple noted violinists of the day refused to play it, again suggesting that the work was poorly written. In the end, those opinions didn't matter much either, for it is now one of the most frequently played and recorded concert pieces; in fact, I've heard his violin concerto almost as often as I've heard his piano concerto, played by some of the top virtuoso performers.

* * * * *

I also love the folk sound of the music of the Central European composers. In particular, two Hungarians did much to put their imprint on their music: Bela Bartok (1881-1945) and his compatriot, Zoltan Kodaly (1882-1967). In a sense, they followed the pattern of the Russians, in that their prime focus was on studying and incorporating the particular musical idioms of their country into their music. They also sought to understand, collect, and promote the folk songs, sounds, and texture of the music of the countryside.

The Hungarians really hit pay dirt when they started researching and recording old Magyar folk melodies, similar to Gypsy music. They scurried around the countryside and collected the music and recorded it wherever they could. Later, more careful research unveiled that the music had direct ties to Asian folk music. The result was a blend of folk music, classicism, and modernism, music that truly reflected the national culture of Hungary, as well as Romania and other countries.

From My Concert Seat

One of the best concert performances I've ever heard of a Bartok work, his *Concerto for Orchestra* (1943), was in the late 1990s, by the New York Philharmonic Orchestra. Prior to that, I was not a big fan of Bartok's music, mostly because it didn't seem to carry the same fulsome sound of, say, Brahms or Tchaikovsky, but that particular performance changed that for me. The piece sounded every bit like a traditional work, almost like a Romantic nineteenth-century work from the old masters.

Recommended Listening

B. Bartok, *Eight Hungarian Folk Songs and Three Romanian Dances*

Z. Kodaly, *Háry János, a Hungarian Folk Opera in 4 Acts* (Authorized shortened version, 1926) and *Dances of Galanta*

Composers weren't the only ones experimenting with new musically artistic forms in the nineteenth century, for painters were too. Like the composers, there were those who believed art should unapologetically express moods and feelings, while others thought a painting should be purely the artist's impressions of how he or she saw and felt nature, a person, an event, or anything captured on a canvas.

Composers were quick to pick up on this, so of course classical music went charging off in yet another direction. This time, it was called impressionism, with no particular program necessary, no rigid format, no big idea to it. The resulting compositions were just their impressions of a scene or something, no more, no less. However, despite all the new experimentation and ideas about where classical music should go, I think it's safe to say that the old masters and their style were far from finished.

CHAPTER 10

A Guide to More of the Romantics

"I gave everything to it I was able to give.
What I have here accomplished, I will never achieve again."
—Camille Saint-Saens,
on composing his famed *"Organ Symphony"*

Anyone who knows art knows the paintings of Cezanne, Monet, and Picasso sparked an art feeding frenzy, of sorts. Even today, on the rare occasion when their works are put up for auction, they still rake in tens of millions. Their paintings are rich in color and intensely engaging, and they intrigue art buyers and those who gawk at them in museums in wide-eyed, mouth-agape amazement. These renowned artists figured out a way to splash their thoughts onto the canvas, to display, through their creations, their perspective on life. It didn't take long for some composers to pick up on this way of looking at things, and their canvas was the musical scale on paper.

In fact, over time, some composers began to think of their music as paintings, artwork of the impressionistic variety. As a result, we were suddenly enlightened with yet another school of thought about what classical music should sound like in the Romantic Era and even whether it should even be called "classical," *per se.*

Clearly, Claude Debussy (France, 1862-1918) should be given credit for getting the ball rolling on this idea, even though he rejected "impressionism" as a term. Debussy took some heat for his famous words: "There is no theory. You merely have to listen. Pleasure is the law." Nevertheless, time proved that he knew what he was talking about. His *Prelude to the Afternoon of a Faun* (1894) typifies the feeling an impressionist composer wants the listener to hear. His *Nocturnes* (1899) expresses a subtle image of nightfall. Remarkable as these are, it was his *La Mer* (1903-05), a ground breaking work filled with imagery, feeling, and the mood of the seascape that jettisoned him into impressionistic musical writing.

From My Concert Seat

I've heard *La Mer* many times, played by orchestras in several different cities I have visited on concert jaunts. It's always the same. I can almost hear the crashing of the waves, the stormy sea, the deceptive tranquility of a gentle wave flowing ashore, the deep, growling echo of the sea's mysterious, menacing depths. Somehow, that sound is absolutely vivid, absolutely graphic. Time and again, Debussy and the impressionists showed in their

works that one does not have to actually live through something or experience it to convey an image of it in the music; the closest Debussy personally got to any ocean was a couple trips across the English Channel!

Debussy acknowledged that one does not have to actually be a ship captain or a career navy man to love the sea or to enable others to feel it or love it through audible perception. As he so aptly expressed, "I have an endless store of memories of the sea, and, to my mind, they are worth more than the reality, whose beauty weighs down thought too heavily."

Imagery in sound was his method of painting, and music was his art. *Estampes* (engravings or prints), and especially his *Images* (1908-12), aim to create a picture of particular images for a listener. *Iberia,* a work within it, is all about Spain, but Debussy only spent one day there, to attend a bullfight. In his works, he defied conventional tonal arrangements and allowed the music to simply flow.

As with any other new trend that catches fire, other composers soon jumped onboard. The following artists, among others, took a cue from Debussy and blended musical imagery to capture the flavor and color of a time, place, or storyline:

Maurice Ravel	France	1875-1937	*Daphnis et Chloé (1912),* not *Bolero*
Isaac Albeniz	Spain	1860-1909	*Iberia (1892)*

Manuel de Falla	Spain	1876-1946	*Nights in the Garden of Spain (1915)*
			The Three Corned Hat (1919)
Frederick Delius	England	1862-1934	*A Summer Night on the River (1911-12)*
Ottorino Respighi	Italy	1879-1936	*The Pines of Rome (1924)*
			The Fountains of Rome (1928)

The influence of Debussy's musical depiction of images is evident in Respighi's *Fountains of Rome* and Albeniz's *Iberia,* their most popular works, both of which I've had the pleasure of enjoying in concert many times. As with *La Mer,* I can almost visualize water fountains, plazas, monuments, and Spanish dances and songs in the colorful melodies of these numbers. The artists of sound were really determined to free their music from the rigid forms of the past, in order to attain a new level of freshness and originality. In Debussy's piano work, *The Joyous Isle* (1904), each part of the piece creates a succession of images that remain distinct. If you listen to it with your eyes closed, you can almost see those images.

Recommended Listening

M. de Falla Spain, *Nights in the Garden of Spain*

Encore

To Cough or Not to Cough?

I bide my time at concerts and wait for the inevitable: the coughing ritual. It starts with one, two, and then a cascade of coughing fits from the audience. I have watched conductors grimace, fidget, go limp for a moment at the podium, or just ignore it until the sound dies down. It's such a ritual that German Comedian Loriot composed what he dubbed *"Coughing Symphony"* as a present for the Berlin Philharmonic's 100th birthday. He said he wanted "to integrate typical concert noises to enrich the work."

The inevitable soon happened. A researcher got in the act and wanted to know the motive behind all the seemingly impromptu coughing. In a 2013 study, University of Hanover Professor Andreas Wagener found that folks cough far more at concerts than anywhere else outside a hospital. He concluded that a lot of it has to do with the music; perhaps the tunes are considered too complex or boring, so the torrent of coughs is actually tied to the music itself. Does his conclusion suggest that coughing is the audience's way of voicing their displeasure at a particular work? Hmm. I'll do a cough meter count during an especially dragging number at a concert someday to see if there's any real truth to that.

* * * * *

There was more to come in the way of innovation in the classical music world in the nineteenth century. This time, it came in a form that could be called crossover music, even a century before the term was invented. This is what the classical biggies had to say about it: Richard Strauss said, "How could I forget the laughing genius of Vienna?" Brahms wrote this about *"Blue Danube"*: "Unfortunately, NOT by Johannes Brahms." He then added, "That man oozes with music!" Wagner surmised, "The most musical mind of Europe."

The old masters weren't falling over themselves about Mozart, Beethoven, or Bach. The man they were talking about was Johann Strauss, the junior (Austria, 1825-99). During the same period when Strauss, Wagner, and Brahms were dominating music, the classical giants of the day, Strauss Jr. was beating the pants off them with an outpouring of music that not only took Europe by storm but also drew thousands of fans and adherents in the U.S. His music was the waltz, and while some classical purists wrinkled their uppity noses and frowned at the very notion that anyone would dare to call it classical, it certainly caught the ear and the attention and admiration of the men who knew good music when they heard it.

Strauss's waltz was admittedly a much easier sell than a standard four-movement symphony. The reason was simple: People could actually dance to it. The purists who scoffed at it and dubbed it "unclassical" certainly missed something.

From My Concert Seat

I knew Tchaikovsky wrote famed waltzes in his perennial favorites, the ballets *Sleeping Beauty* (1889) and *Swan Lake* (1875-76) and especially his *Nutcracker* (1892). Think of the sugarplum fairy waltzing away on stages at Christmastime. However, it took a while for me to figure out that I had actually heard waltz-like melodies in the piano works of Berlioz, Chopin, Schubert, and Ravel. I went back and listened to a few of these works on *YouTube*. Sure enough, there was the waltz!

Richard Strauss thought so much of the other Strauss that he included the lighthearted rhythms and melodies of a Strauss-like waltz in his opera *Der Rosenkavalier (The Cavalier of the Rose)* (1909-10). They are exciting and fun listening, superbly rhythmic. Thus, it was only natural that when the nineteenth-century European highbrow set wanted some music to dance to at their soirees, they turned to the waltz; if the masters endorsed it, so would they. Strauss was there to give them what they wanted, and it was only a matter of time before it moved from the dance floor to the concert hall. The best-known Strauss waltzes, *Blue Danube,* the *Kaiser-Walzer,* and *Tales from the Vienna Woods* are standard numbers on concert bills. *Blue Danube* even turned up in Kubrick's *2001: A Space Odyssey.*

Recommended Listening

J. Strauss, *The Blue Danube Waltz*

* * * * *

Despite all the new-fangled stuff that emerged in the nineteenth century, impressionism, the tone poem, and folk music and dance, the tried-and-true style of the old masters didn't exactly go extinct. Camille Saint-Saens (France, 1835-1921), the widely traveled, musical bon-vivant was every bit the musical child prodigy Mozart was. The ten-year-old Saint-Saens, after finishing playing Mozart's *Piano Concerto No. 15* and a few other pieces, stunned the recital crowd by offering an encore, any one of Beethoven's thirty-two piano sonatas, played entirely from memory, without sheet music.

His five brilliant, colorful piano concertos, and three symphonies, most notably *Symphony No. 3, "Organ Symphony,"* follow to a tee the rigid, standard classical movement forms. Saint-Saens made that very point in his own analysis of the symphony, when he noted that though it was cast in two movements, "the traditional four-movement structure is maintained."

From My Concert Seat

I always remember the night I took my thirteen-year-old daughter to hear the *"Organ Symphony"* at a concert

by the Pasadena Symphony Orchestra. It was the biggest piece after intermission. My daughter and some other kids milled around the big pipe organ, gaping at it. To them, the big organ was the star of the show that night.

A seventeen-year-old Bizet, of *Carmen* fame, stuck to the standard symphony format in his luxuriant, lively, and intensely youthful *Symphony in C* (1855). It was a student work that closely copied the style of his teacher, celebrated musician-composer Charles Gounod, who penned *Symphony in D Major* (1855). The symphony is clearly another case of a student surpassing his teacher. Still, perhaps out of respect for his mentor, Bizet kept his symphony under wraps, and it was never publicly performed while he was alive. Rather, it was discovered eighty years later, in the Paris Conservatory library, and was first played in 1933.

Bizet wasn't the only Frenchman who had a penchant for squirreling his pieces away for ages. Another delightful piece, one I have occasionally heard as sort of a light touch on a concert bill, is Saint Saens's *Carnival of the Animals* (1886). He flatly said he didn't want it played during his lifetime, so the classical world waited a respectable year after his death for a first public performance of it in New York in 1922.

The Russians, however, didn't scrap the old four-movement symphony form. Sergei Prokofiev (1891-1953), Igor Stravinsky (1882-1971), Nikolai Rimsky Korsakov (1844-1908), and Dmitri Shostakovich (1906-75) still wrote nearly all their symphonies, concertos, and chamber works in the traditional four-movement forms. Prokofiev openly paid homage to Haydn's style and format with his *Symphony No. 1, "The Classical"* (1917).

World-acclaimed piano virtuoso, Composer Sergei Rachmaninoff (Russia, 1873-1943), saw the handwriting on the wall for artists after the Bolsheviks seized State power in Russia in 1917. He did what many Russian composers, writers, dancers, and playwrights did after the revolution and got the heck out of there. Eventually, Rachaminoff landed in America, as Prokofiev did for a time and Stravinsky for much longer. Like his two Russian composer expatriates, he did not move one step from the traditional defined movement structure in his three symphonies and four piano concertos.

As an example, there is his *Piano Concerto No. 3* (1909), always billed as one of the toughest piano concertos to play. Actor Geoffrey Rush turned it into a triumph when he struggled to master it in the 1996 film Shine, a bio-pic based on the life of pianist David Helfgott. Rush snagged an Academy Award for best actor for the role.

From My Concert Seat

Though I've heard it played many times by orchestras and soloists, I purposely didn't spotlight Rachmaninoff's crowd favorite, *Rhapsody on a Theme of Paganini* (1934), here. It is undeniably a moving, beautiful, full-throated work, but I have not mentioned it above precisely because it's probably the one work that is recognizable by

many who couldn't care less about classical music. In other words, it sells itself as a showpiece work.

Recommended Listening

N. Rimsky-Korsakov, *Symphony No. 3 in C Major*

* * * * *

Even without Stalin's badgering, hectoring, and demanding that they toe a hard line Soviet line in music, Prokofiev (he returned to the Soviet Union in time) in his seven symphonies and Shostakovich in his fifteen still likely would not have strayed very far from the time-tested models of the past. The most cursory listen to Prokofiev's brooding, tense, yet stirring *Symphony No. 5* premiered in March of 1945, on the verge of the Soviet Union's World War II triumph over Nazi Germany, in the standard symphonic form. It must be said, though, that even a standard four-movement work is no guarantee that some audiences somewhere won't like a symphony, no matter how traditional it seems.

From My Concert Seat

You would have needed a thick parka in balmy Santa Barbara the night the Santa Barbara Symphony played Shostakovich's *Symphony No. 5,* as the chill from the audience was that pronounced. Admittedly, it is no Mozart or

Haydn. I felt I was a minority of one in the audience that night; I absolutely adore the sometimes somber, sometimes stormy sometimes military march-like sound of the symphony. As I heard the tepid applause at the end, though, I realized it was probably best for that orchestra to stick with Mozart next time. That was some years ago, and maybe things would be different today. However, I haven't seen Shostakovich on the bill there since then.

Rimsky-Korsakov's best-known work, *Scheherazade* (1888), is a big-tone, poemesque musical that tells of the old *One Thousand and One Nights* collection of west and south Asian stories and folk tales compiled in Arabic. I'm not sure whether he actually thought of the work as a symphony. Others have dubbed it that, without the pretense of being a formal symphony. Symphony or not, though, it has always been another crowd-pleaser.

It is such a crowd and orchestra favorite that I was amused to see the kids in a youth orchestra at the Aspen Music Festival in July of 2013 when they practically turned the piece into a jam session. The audience got into the spirit of it, so much so that some were bouncing in their seats.

Recommended Listening

S. Prokofiev, *Symphony No. 5 in B Flat Major*

Igor Stravinsky is ranked by many musicologists as a major transformative figure in the history of classical music, a ranking that is well deserved. Stravinsky achieved what Beethoven did with his *"Eroica" Symphony:* He stood the music world on its head with his early path-breaking works. I have heard all three of them in concert over the years: *The Rite of Spring, The Firebird* (1910), and *Petrushka* (1910-11) often in concert over the years. They are primal, raw, driving, and intense, yet they change up with moments of subtle quiescent that provide a respite from the driving sound. It was a revolutionary sound a century ago, when they were composed, and it still is. It came as no surprise that Stravinsky's *The Rite of Spring* caused a scandal and bedlam at its premier at Théâtre des Champs-Élysées on April 2, 1913, in Paris. Stravinsky never stopped talking about that.

In his early and especially his later years, Stravinsky also wrote smaller works, a concerto and two symphonies, such as the *Symphony in C* (1938-40). These are very much in the standard four-movement mode.

Antonin Dvorak (Czechoslovakia, 1841-1904) pretty much followed suit with his nine symphonies, particularly his three big works: *Symphony No. 7,* his "gift to a London audience," as he put it; *Symphony No. 8* (1889); and *Symphony No. 9, "From the New World"* (1893). Whether or not he followed traditional style, these three symphonies are first-rate, big-time pieces that just about every orchestra pencils in on its program during concert season. I've heard them many times, and I'm happy to see that Dvorak has inched his way up the A-list of composers.

* * * * *

Meanwhile, Englishman Elgar's two symphonies have gotten some play. *Symphony No. 1 in A Major* (1908) was used as the theme in the 1984 *Greystoke: The Legend of Tarzan;* generations of graduates have marched in time with his *Pomp and Circumstance March No. 2* to receive their diplomas; and his *Enigma Variations* is the epitome of symphonic décor, if not exactly formal symphonic form. Likewise, Jean Sibelius's (Finland, 1865-1957) seven symphonies, especially his signature *Symphony No. 2,* adhere closely to traditional, old-school models.

From My Concert Seat

I'm always fascinated by how stuff from the old masters keeps popping up even decades after they've been laid to rest. Nearly seventy years after Sibelius's death, some of his previously unheard works were still being discovered. Two, choral works written in 1898, were found on a sheep farm in Finland in 2015.

Recommended Listening

Dvorak, *Symphony No. 7 in D Minor*

Dvorak's *Czech Suite* (1879) and sixteen *Slavonic Dances* (1876, 1886), Prokofiev in his *Lieutenant Kije Suite* (1933), and Sibelius in *Lemminkäinen Suite (Four Legends from the Kalevala)* (1895) have been huge successes because of their emphasis on homegrown folk tales and themes. Sibelius took the patriotic banner to greater lengths in his *Finlandia* (1898). He crowded it with folk, patriotic, and religious themes, partly to thumb his nose at the rule of czarist Russia over Finland, a duchy of Russia before 1917. Shostakovich also gave nods to Russian and Jewish folk music in some of his works; however, they were still solid classicists, and the old masters would have readily recognized that in their works.

Encore

The Gulag...or Worse

At the height of Stalin's terror in the mid-1930s, Shostakovich kept a small bag packed in case of a late-night knock at his door that could land him in front of a firing squad or rotting away for years in the Gulag, a rapping he expected from Stalin's homicidal secret police, the NKVD. By then, Shostakovich had attained fame and renown outside the borders of the Soviet Union, but that alone would not have saved him if Stalin decided his music was hopelessly "anti-Soviet." A few times, he seemed to come close to that peril in Stalin's eyes, but Shostakovich was a survivor. He toed the line when he had to and said, "I began to speak a language incomprehensible to

the people... I know that the party is right." It was anything but, but tragically, that was how things were then, and Shostakovich knew there was no use fighting it.

I can't give Prokofiev a pass either. To go along to get along, he dutifully toed the party line when he had to. There is really no other explanation for writing this pap: *Toasts to Stalin, The Ballad of the Unknown Boy, Guarding the Peace, Ode to the End of the War,* and *Cantata for the Thirtieth Anniversary of the October Revolution.*

Shostakovich, though, was ever the Soviet loyalist, even after Stalin's death in 1953. He paid a glowing musical tribute to the 1905 revolution, the opening gun of the 1917 Bolshevik revolution, in his *Symphony No. 11 in G Minor* Op. 103, subtitled *The Year 1905.* There's the somber, funeral-like sound of the march of the workers to the Winter Palace to petition the czar for just treatment, the gunfire of the troops, and the resultant massacre, set against the screams and shouts of the panicked workers. In the symphony, Shostakovich managed to do his duty to the Soviet State and produce a crackling good, dramatic work complete with gongs, drums, and bugles.

Recommended Listening

D. Shostakovich, *Symphony No. 11 in G Minor "The Year 1905"*

The best that can be said, then, is that the old, standard

symphony did not fade away as the proverbial old soldier did; it just had some new company. There was and has been more new company for the old masters and their music in the twentieth and twenty-first centuries, and there is undoubtedly more to come. However the best company for them then and now was not always in Europe. More than a few Americans also have had their say in the classical music concert halls, but just who are they?

CHAPTER 11

A Guide to America's Classical Greats

"It is becoming increasingly difficult to decide where jazz starts or where it stops, where Tin Pan Alley begins and jazz ends, or even where the borderline lies between classical music and jazz. I feel there is no boundary line."

—Duke Ellington

From My Concert Seat

I didn't see the first concert of this kind that he did, but I did see many others. I'm referring to January 18, 1958, when New York Philharmonic Orchestra Conductor Leonard Bernstein conducted his first Young People's Concert. For the next fourteen years, Bernstein shook up the classical music scene not only by playing the music but also by talking about it to millions of Americans on CBS. In memory of that, I went back and checked out some excerpts on *YouTube* of Bernstein holding forth at the piano while talking to the young people about a particular piece. It's still just as fun and compelling to watch it decades later.

Bernstein didn't just play music for the youth; he ranged over a wide number of musical issues. At the first concert, he asked and answered this question: "What does music mean?" That question was not only asked of youth but of anyone who has ever listened to music, which is everyone. The question is not an esoteric one to wow a youth audience. Rather, it really speaks to the past, present, and, most importantly, the future of music—in this case, classical music in its many new and expanded forms.

Bernstein was undoubtedly well aware that many still think the classical music notables were all born in Italy, Germany, France and England in the eighteenth and nineteenth centuries. Many believe the only composers who did anything of note were European and possibly a few Spaniards thrown in. In taking a stroll through the archives of classical music, it's rather easy to see how such a wrong-headed, short-sighted notion could take root.

Vivaldi, Bach, Mozart, Beethoven, Wagner, Brahms, Tchaikovsky, Mahler, Shostakovich, et. al. are tough acts to follow. American composers who gained international acclaim, such as Aaron Copland and Gershwin, spent a lot of time hanging around European haunts. Thus, American composers have no hope of ever getting their full back-pat in classical musical tradition, not at all the accolades the European giants get. No matter, for in their own way, they have notably expanded the boundaries of the classical sound. They have incorporated jazz, American musical stage sounds, marches, folk, patriotic songs and rhythms, and American literary works in their pieces, and this is no small achievement.

They have written in every one of my list of the major classical music forms: symphonies, concertos, oratorios, overtures, sonatas, operas, tone poems, and quartets. I have heard many works of American composers at concerts. Some, such as Samuel Barber's *Adagio for Strings* (1936), have become set pieces on concert bills. In fact, his *Adagio* has even been crowned as America's and the world's unofficial mourning music, having been played at funerals or to announce the deaths of a plethora of Statesmen and -women and cataclysmic tragedies such as the unforgettable September 11, 2001 terrorist attacks on the U.S.

* * * * *

Many classical music listeners readily recognize these, but I would like to provide a list of the best-known works. I suggest listening to them for a wide range of forms and styles. These composers are and have been very much a part of the classical musical tradition too.

Samuel Barber	(1910-81)	*Adagio for Strings*
		Violin Concerto
Duke Ellington	(1899-1974)	*Sacred Concerts*
Ferde Grofe	(1892-1972)	*Mississippi Suite*
		Grand Canyon Suite

Roy Harris	(1898-1979)	*Symphony No. 3*
		American Symphony
Scott Joplin	(1867-1917)	*Maple Leaf Rag*
		The Entertainer
Aaron Copland	(1900-90)	*Fanfare for the Common Man*
		Appalachian Spring
		Concerto for Piano and Orchestra
George Gershwin	(1898-1937)	*Cuban Overture*
		Rhapsody in Blue
Howard Hanson	(1896-1981)	*Symphony No. 1 in E Minor, "Nordic," Op. 22*
		Lux aeterna, Symphonic Poem for Orchestra with Viola Obligato
		Symphony No. 2 in D-Flat Major, "Romantic," Op. 30
		Symphony No. 7, "A Sea Symphony"
Walter Piston	(1894-1976)	*Symphony No. 2*
		Violin Concerto No. 1
Virgil Thompson	(1896-1989)	*Sonata da Chiesa for instrumental quintet*
		Stabat Mater for soprano and strings
		Filling Station Ballet
		Crossing Brooklyn Ferry for chorus and orchestra

From My Concert Seat

Leonard Bernstein (1918-90) wrote much, much more than his perennial favorite *West Side Story,* even though it is pretty much what most think when they think of Bern-

stein, since it is the most often heard. In fact, he wrote in just about every classical music form. I occasionally hear some of his other works in concert. To get a better feel for the full spectrum of Bernstein as a classical music originator, listen to some or all of these works by him:

Symphony No. 1, "Jeremiah"

Fancy Free* and *Three Dance Variations from "Fancy Free"

Three Dance Episodes from "On the Town"

Symphony No. 2, "The Age of Anxiety" (after W.H. Auden) for Piano and Orchestra

Symphony No. 3, "Kaddish"

American classical composers have not just been copycats of the traditional forms of classical music tradition. They have added a lot of new wrinkles of their own to it. They've helped point the way to the future of classical music with their innovations and add-ons. That future is still evolving and will continue to, as long as there our composers. It is this exciting future, full of potential, with which I will close this guide.

Isang Yun

FINALE

A Guide to the Classical Future

"People who make music together cannot be enemies, at least while the music lasts."
—Paul Hindemith

Like many others, I have asked, "What will the future of classical music hold?" One way to answer that question is to look at some other forms that entered the classical music repertoire in the twentieth century. Two composers who typify the even more radical departure from the past in some of their works are Paul Hindemith (Germany, 1895-1963) and Arnold Schoenberg (Austria, 1876-1953). Both composed standard classical-sounding pieces. Schoenberg, in his earlier phase, composed *Transfigured Night* (1899), a tone poem for string sextet (six instruments). It was deeply influenced by Wagner's *Tristan und Isolde.* To date, I have only heard it on *YouTube.*

Hindemith, on the other hand, composed some works in the traditional form, works such as *Kammermusick* (1922-27), actually a set of eight works for small orchestra and soloists with military marches and dances. However, he was an experimenter and innovator. His best-known works, *Mathis der Maler* (1934) and my personal favorite, *Symphonic Metamorphosis After Themes of Carl Maria Von Weber* (1943) are nearly traditional in classical music form.

From My Concert Seat

I spent much time in a modern-era music lecture series at the Pasadena Music Conservatory one year, grappling with Schoenberg. I must confess it was not a very successful effort, but that wasn't for lack of trying. I really did want to know what the rave was all about. I can say this: The instructor was a big proponent of Schoenberg. She made it plain that while he had many detractors, he started something new, initiated something that couldn't be ignored. I hung in there to learn more, but alas, the jury is still out on how much of it I really absorbed.

Schoenberg was indeed a real musical radical. His big innovation was what has been dubbed "the twelve-tone method." As for the formal definition of this musical system: "The technique is a means of ensuring that all twelve notes of the chromatic scale are sounded as often as one another in a piece of music while preventing the emphasis of any one note through the use of tone rows, orderings of the twelve pitch classes. All twelve notes, thus, give more or less equal importance, and the music avoids being in a key." Admittedly, this is complex stuff, but since Schoenberg invented this type of sound and it ignited yet another revolution in classical music, it is important to see how he explained it in his own words.

For your sake and my own, I'll try to put it in plain English. The twelve-tone method means a piece will likely sound discordant, certainly not a tune you can dance to with any semblance of rhythm. In other words, it doesn't have the standard sound of a work by, say, Mozart or Beethoven. This new system of sound ignited a storm of controversy, as well as some adherents. No one knew better than Schoenberg that there would be a howl over his new sound, and it didn't take long for that howl to bellow.

When he unveiled his big atonal piece, *Five Pieces for Orchestra,* in London in 1912, the audience wasted no time in lighting into it and him. It wasn't really the twelve-tone sound, but that didn't matter. It sounded foreign enough to their ears to spark a chorus of hisses and laughter and lots of puzzled, stupefied looks. Schoenberg took the backlash in stride and even managed to toss out a little self-deprecating humor as a counter. When a stranger who evidently had heard of him but didn't know what he looked like asked, "Are you that Arnold Schoenberg?" he replied with his tongue well up his cheek, "Well, no one else wanted to be, so I had to take the job."

In time, the furor passed, and things settled down. Concert listeners got what they most wanted to hear, what they knew and could recognize as standard fare. You can get the gist of the music that caused the brief uproar by listening to one of Schoenberg's best-known twelve-note compositions, *Variations for Orchestra* (1926-28).This isn't played much in concert, but I've heard it on *YouTube.*

Recommended Listening

P. Hindemith, *Symphonic Metamorphosis After Themes by Carl Maria von Weber*

It's accurate to say that the revolution in musical sound Schoenberg tried to usher in stirred a tidal wave of experimentation in finding new ways of presenting the old sound of classical music. There were also many new faces to present it. Some composed very traditional pieces, while others composed pieces that were bold, brash, and, frankly, way out the box. The new-wave composers latched on to everything they could find to freshen up their sound. They mixed high tech, lights, hard rock music, and natural landscapes, used computers to translate data from magnetic, seismic, and meteorological data into music, and made lots of nods in their music to the hot-button, controversial political issues of the day.

Some of the names are fairly well known, such as German Oliver Messiaen (France, 1908-92). He pushed the classical envelope to the outer limits with his modernist, mystical, mysterious blend of styles that went way beyond innovation and anything even Schoenberg, on his best music-stretching days, ever did. He even weaved his fascination with birds into a number of pieces, including bird sounds into a collection of thirteen pieces for piano *Catalogue d'Oiseaux* (1958) and *La Fauvette des Jardins* (1971).

Karlheinz Stockhausen (Germany, 1928-2007) didn't waste any time when he saw and heard what electronic music could do for classical music in the early 1950s. He soon became the godfather and guru of the sound and turned to electronic music with two *Electronic Studies* (1953, 1954) and two other works that took electronic sound even further into space with his mixed Concrète and electronic work *Gesang der Jünglinge* (1955-56). It sounded so far out that it prompted one commentator to say it was "music that no psychedelic band could ever surpass."

Messianen's and Stockhausen's works pop up fairly often on concert bills, but I've only heard excerpts from their works on *YouTube*. I have to steel myself for them.

From My Concert Seat

It's confession time again. I've had to come to grips with a brutal reality about myself and classical music. While I am always willing to give a listen to the works of contemporary composers, I am still very much attached to the old masters. So deeply are they ingrained in my musical psyche that it's tough to move past them in my preferred listening.

I have suggested to some orchestra PR folk that they

offer more of the works of contemporary composers as separate showcases for the new music on a concert bill once or twice during the concert season. This would better accustom classical music listeners to their often eclectic blending of new and old sounds and styles. The way it's usually done now is to plop one of the new pieces at the top of a concert bill and hope it has some resonance, but that really doesn't seem to do much for me or anyone else.

Pulitzer Prize-winning Composer John Adams made a statement on the horrendous shock, tragedy, and soul-searching Americans experienced in the aftermath of the September 11 terrorist attacks in Washington and New York in his choral work, *On the Transformation of Souls.* Adams was hardly alone in weaving political controversy and themes into classical compositions that raised eyebrows and got tongues wagging. Mark Anthony Turnage's *Blood on the Floor* and Frederic Rzewski's *Coming Together* stirred intense controversy with their out-front political themes. South Korean Composer Unuk Chin mixes electronic and acoustic sounds; she did it with spectacular effect in her opera. *Alice in Wonderland.*

Thomas Ades got even more creative, or at least more bizarre, when he parlayed his accidental trigger of the security system in a building into an orchestral work titled *These Premises Are Alarmed.* If Strauss or Liszt could find all sorts of mythical characters and scenarios on which to base their tone poems, then Ades's inspiration from a burglar alarm is just as good as any.

There is also the ghost, or at least a shade, of Debussy in some of the works by the more contemporary classical composers such as John Cage (America, 1912-92). He wrote sonatas, piano interludes, and works based on the ancient Chinese text of the *I Ching*, but he really hit pay dirt with his Debussy-like *In a Landscape*, a series of pieces written from 1939 to 1952. They used many instruments, including: muted piano, and cymbal tin cans, conch shell, ratchet, bass drum, buzzers, water gong, metal wastebasket, lion's roar and amplified coil of wire for tin cans, muted gongs, audio frequency oscillators, variable speed turntables with frequency recordings and recordings of generator whines, amplified coil of wire, amplified *marimbula* (a Caribbean instrument similar to the African thumb piano), and electric buzzer for magnetic tape recording of any forty-two phonograph records.

* * * * *

Not a lot of old-style, composer-conductors in the mode of Mendelssohn and Strauss remain, but that fine art didn't die in the nineteenth century either. Former Los Angeles Philharmonic Conductor Esa Pekka Solanon (Finland, 1958-present) has blended old-school traditional forms with a lot of the modernist experimental styling in his works, including *...auf Den Ersten Blick und Ohne Zu Wissen...* (1980, a saxophone concerto with a title taken from Franz Kafka's *The Trial), Floof* for soprano and ensemble (1982, on texts by

Stanisław Lem), and the orchestral *L.A. Variations* (1996).

In my personal opinion, it is a real compliment to classical music that it has been valued enough to be kept, expanded, stretched, broadened, transformed, bent, and even redefined. I cite one important example to show how things both change and stay the same in how we view and define classical music: Art music is that example. I noted earlier that art music, broadly defined, is music that's valued for its own sake, music of thought, depth, and expressiveness. It is continually played as standard repertoire of the classics. When I think of art music, I think of classical music.

The new trends have broadened out the traditional view of what's categorized as "art music." It now includes jazz, folk, and musicals, as well as music from other cultures, such as Asian, African, and Latin American. Jazz in particular offers a number of works that are now considered art music, classics by Ellington, John Coltrane, Miles Davis, Charlie Parker, and Dizzy Gillespie. These are only a few of the towering figures in jazz who have become household names in the classical music tradition.

Recommended Listening

John Coltrane, *A Love Supreme Live*

Pop culture has and will continue to have a huge impact on art music. Rap, reggae, and even musicals, from *STOMP to Les Miserables* and many other artwork musicals, have become staples of the classic genre. Mixed media and digital music from Africa and Asia will also become more integrated into the art music scene.

I can say with certainty that there will be lots of crossover music, blended musical sounds from the classics, rock, and reggae. In the 1960s, The Beatles, with *Sgt. Pepper's Lonely Heart Club Band,* and in the 1970s, Miles, with his groundbreaking *Bitches Brew* and Marvin Gaye's *What's Going On?* all set new standards for musical sound innovation, creativity, and freshness. Surely, more artists will borrow from and build on the tradition of originality and innovation and will use everything from social media to *YouTube* to embed their sounds into the classical/art music genre, just as the Baroque ushered in an age of new instruments, styles, and musical models that carried into opera, the symphony, and solo works.

That, in turn, morphed into tone poems, programmatic music, the intensely personal introspective impressionism, and from there the experiments with atonality. I've tried to show that it didn't stop there; instead, it stretched the definition of classical music to pieces in jazz, folk, rock, R&B, and just about anything that has sound and an enduring shelf life. If any one composer could understand and applaud that kind of development, it would be Beethoven.

* * * * *

That ancient glass-half-full vs. glass-half-empty conundrum is not just a trite cliché, especially when examining the state of women and persons of color in classical music in the twenty-first Century. As for the half-empty, ethnic and gender diversity still remains a troublesome question for American orchestras. Just over 4 percent of these musicians are African-American and Latino, according to the League of American Orchestras, and when it comes to orchestra boards and CEOs, the numbers are even starker: Minorities are truly that, making up only 1 percent. Ethnic diversity is also a rare sight among guest soloists and conductors. The number of African-American and Hispanic students at the nation's top music institutes aren't much better, as these make up a small fraction of the students at the elite academies.

A study in February of 2015 by Kings College London's Christina Scharff found extensive inequalities at every level of the classical music profession in regard to sex, class, education, and ethnicity. Among its findings: The proportion of women working in the arts and cultural sector has fallen to 43 percent; women earn less than men (£29,015, compared to £34,669).

From My Concert Seat

The conductor is the jewel in the orchestral crown. In the twenty-year period between 1995 and 2015, I saw more than 100 conductors of big and small orchestras. Among all of these, I could count on one hand and one finger the number of African-American, American-, His-

panic, or South American-born Latin conductors, and female conductors. The scorecard reads exactly two women, two African-American conductors (one of whom was the late, great James DePriest) and two Hispanics.

As for the half-full part: I'm thrilled that women and Asian musicians are doing better in terms of numbers in orchestras, chorales, and smaller ensembles. Isang Yun (Korea, 1917-95) was another virtual composing machine. He's written in all forms: operas, symphonies, and concertos, duets, trios, quartets, quintets, and various chamber arrangements. His major works are *Concerto for Violoncello and Orchestra* (1975-76) and the *Violin Concerto No. 1* (1981). From 1982 to 1987, he wrote a cycle of five symphonies: *Symphony No. 1* in four movements (1982-83); *Symphony No. 2* in three movements (1984); *Symphony No. 3* in one movement (1985); *Symphony No. 4 "Im Dunkeln Singen"* in two movements (1986); and *Symphony No. 5* for high baritone and orchestra in five movements (Nelly Sachs, 1987). He blended traditional classical forms with folk and experimental.

In April of 2015, I considered it a great privilege and a pleasure to promote on my Pacifica Radio show the West Coast performance of the *Water Passion After St. Matthew* by the Los Angeles Master Chorale at Disney Hall. It's a work by Tan Dun (China, 1957). Dun has also written *Concerto for Orchestra* (2002) and *Concerto for Guitar and Orchestra* (1996). Toru Takimitsu (Japan, 1930-96) has two widely acclaimed works, *Quatrain* for clarinet, violin, cello, piano and orchestra (1977), and *In an Autumn Garden* for gagaku orchestra (1973). Their works have been performed by major orchestras in Europe, America, and Asia.

Classical music orchestras are more gender- and ethnic-diverse than ever before. There are more female and minority conductors, and depending on the concert bill, the classical concert audiences are far more diverse. There are no visible barriers to any woman or composer of color from composing, publishing, or even receiving the occasional commission to perform their works.

This is my hope for the future. As the century progresses and more minorities and women rise to positions of power and influence in Western society, the classical music world will not remain the forbidden enclave it has pretended to be for three centuries, from the Baroque to the modern era. Just as classical music has never been the sole preserve of white males in the centuries past, when it was thought to be and regarded as such, back when talented women and people of color were pushed to the deep recesses of the classical music world, they were still there writing, performing, and stamping their imprint on the music.

In the twenty-first century these will proudly burst out of that recess and become a bigger part of the driving, inspiring, and creative force that has always been the trademark of classical music. The classical music world will be even better for it.

This is the world that Beethoven opened for me, and I hope this book has opened it for you.

From My Concert Seat: The Curtain Closes

On May 12, 2015, I was reminded once more of the profound power of classical music to trumpet the universal spirit of humanity. The occasion was a concert by the Armenian National Philharmonic Orchestra, billed as "A Concert of Remembrance" on the 100th anniversary of the estimated 1 million Armenian victims of the 1915 Turkish-initiated holocaust. The concert was moving, emotional, and often tearful. The orchestra, with its impassioned playing of Armenian composers Aram Khachaturian's *Spartacus Suite* (1955-57) and Tigran Masurian's *Violin Concerto* captured all the sorrow, pathos, memory, and vision of hope a century later of yet another of the world's grotesque genocidal outrages inflicted on an innocent people.

As I listened to the music, I thought, "What better way to commemorate the suffering of a people whose spirit remained unbroken than with this music?" It proved again that classical music can and has been both a beacon of monumental hope and a source of magnificent enlightenment in a world that has, at times throughout the ages, been desperately short of both. It is one more reason I sing the praises of classical music, just as I did again that night.

A Guide to the Classical Jargon

Aria. This is an impassioned song in which soprano, tenor, or bass can be heard within an opera production. Some very creative individuals figured out that an aria can also be for a solo instrument too; Bach spruced up parts of his piano sites with an aria.

Cadenza. This is how a concert virtuoso performer really shows off his or her stuff. The soloist can deviate from the score. The chords and notes can be written for them, or they may write their own and take off on any flight of musical fancy that suits them. That flight can last for a few seconds to several minutes. Meanwhile, the orchestra and conductor wait patiently for them to finish, then jump back in.

Canon. This is a piece of music in which two or more voices (instrumental parts) sing or play the same music, starting at different times. A lot of filmgoers got their first introduction to the canon in the 1980 movie, *Ordinary People,* which Robert Redford earned an Academy Award for directing. The music was the epitome of a gentle, soft, easygoing work. It was *The Canon and Gigue for 3 Violins and Basso*

Continuo by German Baroque composer Johann Pachelbel (1653-1706).

Cantata. This is a short oratorio.

Concerto Grosso. This is Italian for "big concert," though the piece is not always for a big ensemble. There are small ensemble concerto grossi (the plural), with the soloists tossing the music to the orchestra.

Continuous Bass Basso Continuo. This keeps the bass line going with a keyboard instrument and another bass instrument such as cello, violone (an old form of double-bass), or bassoon.

Counterpoint. This is absolutely crucial to music, so the definition bears repeating. If you play one melody simultaneously with another, they are playing counter to each other. This is contrapuntal or, more commonly, counterpoint. Think of two dueling singers going at each other at the same time. All composers since then have genuflected to Bach for this; he is the absolute king of the hill of counterpoint

Dissonance. This literally means a harsh, disagreeable combination of sounds; discord. Music dissonance expresses the jumble of human emotions in sound, a sound that can grate on the nerves of some.

Duets. This is two singers going back and forth.

Key. This is the main note of a piece on a scale of pitches. If you see a symphony in the key of D, the main note is the D note.

Libretto. This is the text of the opera.

Madrigal. This is a secular vocal number with no instruments, for anywhere from two to eight singers.

Major and Minor Keys. This is the note scale that starts a composition: in "C Minor" or "A Major" and so on. Another way of thinking of it is to remember that the major keys tend to make a happy sound, while the minor keys are more morose.

Melody. This is music that moves in a straight line, one note after another.

Movement. This is a self-contained part of a musical composition or musical form. You'll see and hear a symphony referred to as "first movement," "second movement," and so on.

Motet. This is a choral piece of music for a church service that's sung without any instruments.

Partita. This is a piece of a single instrument or multiple instruments.

Recitative. This is like talking without music. Rap is recitative, for example, but for our purposes, it's a predominant form in opera and religious verses, one in which the singer talks between numbers.

Rondo. This is a musical theme that returns over and over and contrasts with another theme.

Scherzo. This is a quick-paced, frolicking sound, sometimes called musically humorous.

Notes

Introduction: Beethoven and Me: A Beginner's Guide to Classical Music

Alexander Wheelock Thayer provides a physical description of Beethoven in Thayer's *Life of Beethoven, Book 1 Revised,* Elliot Forbes, ed. (Princeton, NJ: Princeton University Press; Revised edition, 1991).

For a virtual note by note analysis of Beethoven's *Seventh Symphony,* see, Gutmann, Peter, Classical Notes http://www.classicalnotes.net/classics4/beethovenseventh.html.

A good summary of how musicians differ with each other on their music see, *When It Comes To Interpreting Music, Classical Musicians Have No Constitution* http://www.blogiversity.org/blogs/the_horn/archive/2011/11/23/when-it-comes-to-interpreting-music-classical-musicians-have-no-constitution.aspx.

Mawer, Deborah, in *The Ballets of Maurice Ravel: Creation and Interpretation* (Farnham, Surrey, UK: Ashgate Publishing Co., 2006), 224 recounts the spat between Toscanini and Ravel over how Bolero should be played.

Horton, Andrew J., provides a detailed look at Stalin's definition of Socialist realism in, "The Forgotten Avant

Garde: Soviet Composers Crushed by Stalin," *Central European Review,* Vol. 1, No. 28, June, 1999.

OVERTURE: A GUIDE TO MY FAVORITE CLASSICAL TERMS

Leonard Bernstein devoted one of his Young People's Concert lectures to the sonata. It's still one of the best discussions of this musical form. http://www.leonardbernstein.com/ypc_script_what_is_sonata_form.htm.

For a full discussion on the history of the quartet see, *Classic Cat* http://www.classiccat.net/iv/stringquartet.info.php.

One of the more comprehensive looks at the history of the oratorio is Howard Smither's *The History of the Oratorio.* Vol. 1-4, (Chapel Hill, NC: University of North Carolina Press, 1977-2000).

Blom, Eric, "Overture." *Grove's Dictionary of Music and Musicians,* fifth edition, edited by Eric Blom, (Toronto, Canada: Macmillan Publishers, 1954).

"More than Just A Pretty Overture: Rossini's 'William Tell'." *NPR Music,* August 12, 2011.

Spencer, Piers, ed. Allison Latham, "Symphonic poem [tone-poem]." *The Oxford Companion to Music* (Oxford and New York: Oxford University Press, 2002).

There are many works on the concerto, but the most concise piece on this is the excerpt by David Pogue and Scott Speck, from their *Classical Music For Dummies,* "Understanding Concertos in Classical Music" from http://www.

dummies.com/how-to/content/understanding-concertos-in-classical-music.html.

There are an endless number of books on opera and the operas of the leading opera composers. The one I found most useful was Fred Plotkin's *Opera 101: A Complete Guide to Learning and Loving Opera* (New York: Hatchette Books, 1994).

Shankar Vedantam, "Do Orchestras Really Need Conductors," November 27, 2012, http://www.npr.org/blogs/deceptivecadence/2012/11/27/165677915/do-orchestras-really-need-conductors.

There's also a vast literature on the symphony too. However, for a basic primer on it, see Michael Steinberg's *The Symphony: A Listener's Guide* (London: Oxford University Press, 1998).

Chapter 1: A Guide to the Baroque

For the dictionary definition of the Baroque see: http://www.merriam-webster.com/dictionary/baroque.

I found Manfred F. Bukofzer's *Music in the Baroque Era: From Monteverdi To Bach* one of the best primers on Baroque music, its composers, and their influence (Freiberg, Germany: Von Elterlein Press, 2014).

Two books that provide an excellent, abbreviated overview of Italian and French opera during the Baroque period are Donald Grout and Hermine Weigel's *A Short History of Opera,* 4th Edition (New York: Columbia University Press, 2003); and Caroline Wood and Graham Sadler's *French Ba-*

roque Opera: A Reader, (Farnham, Surrey, UK: Ashgate Publishing Co., 2000).

The Famous People Website provides a brief bio of Lully, http://www.thefamouspeople.com/profiles/jean-baptiste-lully-458.php.

Though there is no full biography on the life and work of Barbara Strozzi, there is much material on her in scattered music history readers. See Rosand, Ellen "The Voice of Barbara Strozzi," in Jane Bowers and Judith Tick's *Women Making Music: the Western Art Tradition, 1150-1950* (Urbana, Ill.: University of Illinois Press, 1986) 168–190.

CHAPTER 2: A GUIDE TO AFRICAN-AMERICAN CLASSICAL COMPOSERS

Abdul, Raoul, *Blacks in Classical Music, A Personal History* (New York: Dodd, Mead & Company, 1977).

For the full story of "goin' home" from Dvorak's *New World Symphony,* see http://www.americanmusicpreservation.com/GoinHome.htm.

For a detailed look at the work and achievements of blacks in classical music, see: http://www.blackpast.org/perspectives/black-composers-and-musicians-classical-music-history.

The list of classical works influenced by jazz is compiled at: http://en.wikipedia.org/wiki/List_of_jazz-influenced_classical_compositions.

See "Ignatio Sancho" http://en.wikipedia.org/wiki/Ignatius_Sancho.

The Beethoven-Bridgetower saga is fully detailed at: http://en.wikipedia.org/wiki/George_Bridgetower#Meeting_with_Beethoven.

Africlassical.com offers much useful information on Coleridge–Taylor and other black classical musician-composers, http://chevalierdesaintgeorges.homestead.com/song.html.

Smith, Catherine Parsons, *William Grant Still: A Study in Contradictions* (Berkeley: University of California, 2000).

See Bio.com for a short biography of Florence Price http://www.biography.com/people/florence-beatrice-price-21120681.

Hasse, John Edward, *Beyond Category: The Life and Genius of Duke Ellington* (New York: Simon & Schuster, 1993).

William Robin, "Great Divide at the Concert Hall: Black Composers Discuss the Role of Race," *New York Times,* August 8, 2014.

Chapter 3: A Guide to More Baroque

Vivaldi's influence on Bach and other composers has been detailed in several books on his life and work. The most recent is Michael Talbot's *Vivaldi* (NY: Oxford University Press, 2000). The quip by Stravinsky on Vivaldi can be found in The Talk Classical On Line Forum http://www.talkclassical.com/23275-vivaldi-1-concerto-400-a.html.

The quotes by Brahms, Mozart, and Beethoven on Handel and Bach are in Burkholder, Peter J. Grout, Donald Jay and Paslisca, Claudia A., *A History of Western Music,* 8th

Edition (New York: W.W. Norton & Company, Inc., 2010).

There are numerous biographies on Bach and Handel, as well as many studies on their works and their influence on Western music. These two provided the most up-to-date look at their life and works: Winton Dean, *Handel's Operas, 1726-1741* (Woodridge: Boydell, 2006) and Peter F. Williams, *The Life of Bach* (Cambridge: Cambridge University Press, 2004).

Maev Kennedy, "Jimi Hendrix and Handel: Housemates separated by time," *The Guardian,* May 10, 2010.

I relied on Burkholder, Grout, and Palisca's *A History of Western Music,* 8th Edition, 403-411, 414, 428 and 511-517 for the thumbnail sketches of Domenico Scarlatti, Francois Couperin and Dieterich Buxtehude's influence and their works.

On the students who replicated Bach' s walk, see: "Students to honor J.S. Bach and Reenact Moravian History with Walk to New York," http://www.moravian.edu/default.aspx?pageid=526.

For bios and assessments of the works of Bach's musical sons, see: Carus-Verlag Online http://www.carus-verlag.com/index.php3?BLink=ID3e6222f0d4c9b&selSprache=1.

There are sections on them in *A History of Western Music,* 8th Edition, 437, 440-441, 442, 522-24, 550.

Chapter 4: A Guide to Hispanic Classical Composers

See "The Greatest Spanish Composers: Maestros of Spain's Fiery Musical Heritage," http://www.favorite-classical-composers.com/spanish-composers.html.

Garland, Peter, *In Search of Silvestre Revueltas, Essays 1978-1990* (Santa Fe: Soundings, 1991).

For a complete list of other important Latin American classical composers, see: Janelle Gelfand, *The Cincinnati Enquirer,* August 7, 2002, http://www.enquirer.com/editions/2002/08/07/tem_latin_composers.html.

Mexico has a long, rich tradition in classical music. Its composers have gained greater recognition in recent years for their unique use of the folk and Indian songs, rhythms, dances, and instruments of Mexico in their music. Their works are increasingly turning up on concert bills in the U.S. and other countries. See: James Baker's "Mexican Classical Music: From the Known to the Unknown," http://tpr.org/post/mexican-classical-music-known-unknown December 15. 2013.

"List of Mexican Composers of Classical Music," http://en.wikipedia.org/wiki/List_of_Mexican_composers_of_classical_music.

Parker, Robert L., *Carlos Chavez: Mexico's Modern-Day Orpheus* (Boston: Twayne, 1983).

Chapter 5: A Guide to the Three Giants

One could write a book just on the books, articles, and scholarly studies on the lives, works, and influence of Haydn, Mozart, and Beethoven in the world of music and beyond. To give an idea of how vast the library of literature is on the three men, the definitive *A History of Western Music,* 8th Edition alone has ten columns of listings of the various books and studies on them.

The three most recent are: A. Peter Brown, *The Symphonic Repertoire, Vol.2: The First Golden Age of the Viennese Symphony: Haydn, Mozart, Beethoven and Schubert* (Bloomington: Indiana University Press, 2002), David Wyn Jones, ed. *Haydn,* (Oxford: Oxford University Press, 2002); Hermann Albert, *W.A. Mozart* (New Haven: Yale University Press, 2007) ; and Lewis Lockwood, *Beethoven: The Music and the Life* (New York: Norton, 2003).

One writer got especially creative with Beethoven and wrapped a narrative of the composer around the odd odyssey of a lock of his hair that was pilfered from his head on his deathbed. I read the book twice, and his hair did indeed take a fascinating journey. See: Russell Martin, *Beethoven's Hair: An Extraordinary Historical Odyssey and Musical Mystery Solved* (London: Bloomsbury, 2000).

Limelight Magazine has a good piece on how symphonies got their nicknames, http://www.limelightmagazine.com.au/Article/272097,classical-music-s-most-famous-nicknames-explained.aspx.

Mozart actually dedicated six quartets to Haydn. See:

http://www.prestoclassical.co.uk/w/49998/Wolfgang-Amadeus-Mozart-Six-Quartets-dedicated-to-Haydn-Quartets-14-19.

For a good source discussion on Mozart's "A Musical Joke" see: "The Music of Sound" http://whyfiles.org/114music/2.html.

On the Beethoven and Haydn relationship, see: John Suchet, http://www.classicfm.com/composers/beethoven/

guides/beethoven-and-haydn-their-relationship.

The *"Eroica" Symphony* is such a dominant force in classical musical literature and history that there's a website on it alone: http://www.beethovenseroica.com/Pg2_hist/history.html.

I love the story of how Haydn supposedly got on his knees every night and beseeched God to let him finish *The Creation.* It may be apocryphal, but of his deeply religious bent there is no doubt. Mark Berry does an entire piece on Haydn, his works, and its place in theology. See Haydn's "Creation' and Enlightenment Theology," http://www.academia.edu/267334/Haydn_s_Creation_and_Enlightenment_Theology.

Chapter 6: A Guide to Women Composers

There's an excellent assessment of the works of and cool reception to the music Fanny Mendelssohn Hensel and Clara Schumann in *A History of Western Music,* 8th Edition, 612-13, 618-19, 632, 651-52, 653.

Clara Schumann's quote on the role of women can be found at: http://en.wikipedia.org/wiki/Clara_Schumann.

For a fairly comprehensive look at Amy Beach's life and work, see: http://en.wikipedia.org/wiki/Amy_Beach.

The full schedule of the British Academy panel on "Women in Classical Music" can be found at: http://basca.org.uk/basca-events/women-in-classical-music/.

John Benson, "How One Woman Is Bridging The Gap

Between Classical Music And Latinos," *Huffington Post,* October 18, 2013.

Rosi Pentreath, "Six of the best: contemporary female composers," http://www.classical-music.com/article/six-best-contemporary-female-composers, March 4, 2015.

CHAPTER 7: A GUIDE TO OPERA

Tom Huizenga gives an amusing, informative take on bel canto singing in "Talk Like An Opera Geek: Savoring The Bel Canto Sound," March 28, 2012, http://www.npr.org/blogs/deceptivecadence/2012/03/28/149524661/talk-like-an-opera-geek-savoring-the-bel-canto-sound.

Patrick Barbier provides a detailed look at the gruesome but popular practice of castrating young boys in opera singing in the seventeenth and eighteenth centuries in *The World of the Castrati: The History of an Extraordinary Operatic Phenomenon* (London: Souvenir Press, 1998).

Pistone, Daniele, *Nineteenth Century Italian Opera from Rossini to Puccini* (Portland: Amadeus, 1995); Budden, Julian, *Verdi,* 3rd ed., (Oxford: Oxford University Press, 2008).

"Coretta Scott King, Interview, " June 12, 2004, http://www.achievement.org/autodoc/page/kin1int-1

Charlton, David, *Gretry and the Growth of Opera-comique* (Cambridge: Cambridge University Press, 1986).

Lesley Nelson-Burns gives an excellent short history of Gay's "Beggar's Opera" in "The Contemplator's Short History of John Gay and the Beggar's Opera," http://www.contemplator.com/history/johngay.html.

Susan McClary zeroes in on the portrayal of women in Carmen set against attitudes toward women in nineteenth-century France and indeed beyond in *Georges Bizet: Carmen* (New York: Cambridge University Press, 1992).

Wagner: The Complete Epic with Richard Burton and Vanessa Redgrave, 4 disc set, 466 minutes, re-released on DVD, 2005 on Amazon.

I took this quote by Wagner on Wagner from "The Artwork of the Future" in *A History of Western Music,* 8th Edition, 692.

Wagner's anti-Semitic utterances have been well documented. See: Jacob Katz's, *The Darker Side of Genius: Richard Wagner's Anti-semitism* (Hanover, N.H.: University Press of New England, 1986). Wagner's ugly anti-semitism carried over to his heirs. I read Wagner's great grandson Gottfried Wagner's book, *Twilight of the Wagners: The Unveiling of a Family's Legacy in 1999,* (New York: Picador, 1999). It gives a revealing look at how they cozied up to Hitler.

There are also reams of studies and many books on Wagner's life and music. Of the major biographies on him, I found the most useful was *Richard Wagner, The Last of the Titans* (New Haven: Yale University Press, 2004).

The Jessyne Norman Collection, Phillips, Audio CD (November 8, 2005).

Chapter 8: A Guide to the Soloist

Todd, Larry R., *Mendelssohn: A Life in Music* (Oxford: Oxford University Press, 2003).

Groves and Sullivan "discover" Schubert: http://en.wikipedia.org/wiki/George_Grove.

Newbould, Brian, *Schubert: the Music and the Man* (Berkeley: University of California Press, 1997).

Hans Gal spends much time looking at Schubert's *Unfinished Symphony* from many angles in "The Riddle of Schubert's Unfinished Symphony," http://www.hansgal.com/storage/writings/riddle.pdf.

Szulc, Tad, *Chopin in Paris: The life and Times of the Romantic Composer* (New York: DaCapo, 2000).

John Worthen details Schumann's life, mental torments, and his music in *Robert Schumann: Life and Death of a Musician* (New Haven: Yale University Press, 2007).

A concise biography of Franz Liszt's life and piano virtuosity is Dana Gooley's, *The Virtuoso Liszt* (Cambridge: Cambridge University Press, 2004).

"How Franz Liszt Became the World's First Rock Star," *NPR,* October 22, 2011

Ledbetter, David, *Bach's Well-Tempered Clavier: The 48 Preludes and Fugues* (New Haven: Yale University Press, 2002); Plantings, Leon, *Beethoven's Concertos: History, Style, Performance* (New York: Norton, 1999).

Kramer, Richard, *Distant Cycles: Schubert and the Conceiving of Song* (Chicago; University of Chicago Press, 1994); Finson, Jon W., Robert Schumann, *The Book of Songs* (Cambridge Mass.: Harvard University Press, 2008); Reid, Paul, *The Beethoven Song Companion* (Manchester, U.K.: Manchester University Press, 2007).

Chapter 9: A Guide to the Romantics

On the alleged Wagner and Brahms feud, see: http://en.wikipedia.org/wiki/War_of_the_Romantics.

Frisch, Walter, *Brahms: The Four Symphonies* (New Haven: Yale University Press, 2003).

Watson, Derek, *Bruckner* (New York: Oxford University Press, 1996).

Cooke, Deryck, *Gustav Mahler: An Introduction to His Music* (London: Faber & Faber, 1980); On the virulent anti-semitism that Mahler faced and how he and other Jewish artists and intellectuals of the nineteenth century dealt with it at the price of their religion, see: Francesca Draughon and Raymond Knappe's "Gustav Mahler and the Crisis of Jewish Identity,' http://www.echo.ucla.edu/Volume3-issue2/knapp_draughon/knapp_draughon1.html.

Jones, David Wyn, *Beethoven, Pastoral Symphony* (New York: Cambridge University Press, 1995); see: https://www.cantonsymphony.org/423 for a discussion of Mendelssohn's two "program" symphonies, *The Italian* and *The Scottish.*

Richardson, Brian, *Berlioz, Symphonie Fantastique* (Leeds: Mayflower, 1990).

Kennedy, Michael, Richard Strauss, *Man, Musician, Enigma* (Cambridge: Cambridge University Press, 1999); On Strauss's very dubious relationship with Hitler, see: Michael H. Kater's, "Music; Richard Strauss and Hitler's Reich: Jupiter in Hell," *New York Times,* January 6, 2002.

On the impact of Liszt's tone poems, see: Classical Net,

http://www.classical.net/music/recs/reviews/fenech/Liszt-SymPoem.php, and for Franck's music and tone poem, see: "Franck, César." *Norton/Grove Concise Encyclopedia of Music*. (Pub. in UK as Grove Concise Dictionary of Music.). (New York: Norton, 1988).

Green, Richard, *Holst: the Planets* (Cambridge: Cambridge University Press, 1995); Powell, Neil, *Benjamin Britten, A Life for Music* (NY: Henry Holt, 2013) ; Kennedy, Michael, *The Life of Elgar* (Cambridge: Cambridge University Press, 2004).

For a short biography on Bedrich Smetna and an assessment of the Moldau, see: *Bookspan, 101 Masterpieces of Music and Their Composers,* 379-80.

Benestad, Finn, et. al., Edvard Grieg, *The Man and the Artist* (Lincoln: University of Nebraska Press, 1998).

For a short history on the "mighty five" Russian composers and their mission to promote Russian folk culture in their music see, *A History of Western Music,* 8th Edition, 714-720.

There are many works on Tchaikovsky's music as well as speculation about his homosexuality and what, if any, effect it had on his music and personal life. Anthony Holden's *Tchaikovsky: A Biography* (New York: Random House, 1995) covers much of that ground.

Suchoff, Benjamin, *Bela Bartok: Life and Work* (Lanham, Md.: Scarecrow, 2001).

Chapter 10: A Guide to More of the Romantics

Nichols, Roger, *The Life of Debussy* (Cambridge: Cambridge University Press, 1998); Debussy gives his ideas on music and its meaning especially impressionism in *Debussy on Music: The Critical Writings of the Great French Composer,* Francois Lesure ed., (New York: Knopf, 1977). The other impressionist composers, Isaac Albeniz and Manuel de Falla, are discussed in *A History of Western Music,* 8th Edition, 797; Everything anyone wants to know about Respighi can be found on the website of the Respighi Society: http://www.musicweb-international.com/respighi/.

For background on Frederick Delius, see: http://en.wikipedia.org/wiki/Frederick_Delius.

The most recent biography of Maurice Ravel is Benjamin Ivry's *Maurice Ravel: A Life* (New York: Welcome Books, 2000).

"What's Behind the Coughing at Classical concerts?" Desutsch Welle.

http://www.dw.de/whats-behind-the-coughing-at-classical-concerts/a-16652527, March 22, 2013.

The man known as the waltz king, Johann Strauss Jr.'s, biggest admirers were the other Strauss, Wagner, and Brahms. Their admiring quotes on him are found at: http://en.wikipedia.org/wiki/Johann_Strauss_II#Musical_rivals_and_admirers.

The waltzes in R. Strauss's opera *Der Rosenkavalier* are

discussed in http://en.wikipedia.org/wiki/Johann_Strauss_II.

See: http://en.wikipedia.org/wiki/Symphony_in_C_(Bizet) for the full story on the strange odyssey of Bizet's schoolboy symphony.

Martin Bookspan gives the very underrated Camille Saint-Saens who composed one of my favorites, "*Organ Symphony,*" and many other excellent piano works a full assessment in *101 Masterpieces of Music & Their Composers* (New York: Doubleday, 1968) 318-326.

Norris, Geoffrey, *Rachmaninoff* (Oxford: Oxford University Press, 2001).

Barnett, Andrew, *Sibelius* (New Haven: Yale University Press, 2007).

The literature on Stravinsky is voluminous. There are two columns of works on him listed in *A History of Western Music,* 8th Edition. There are countless articles that recount the storm that broke when *The Rite of Spring* was premiered in Paris in 1913. However, the one biography that is fairly comprehensive on his life and work is Stephen Walsh's *The New Grove Stravinsky* (New York: Grove, 2002).

Bookspan, on Rimsky-Korsakov and Scheherazade in *101 Masterpieces of Music & Their Composers,* 312-317.

Sibelius, "Two Choral Pieces Rediscovered," http://sibeliusone.com/2015/03/two-choral-pieces-rediscovered/, March 20, 2015.

Beckerman, Michael B., *New Worlds of Dvorak: Searching in America for the Composer's Inner Life* (New York: Norton, 2003).

The woeful tale of the torments Stalin inflicted on Russian artists, especially Shostakovich and, to a lesser extent, Prokofiev, has been the subject of many books and articles on the Soviet Union in the 1930s to the 1950s under Stalin. The two books on both composers that assess their works and their peril are Harlow Robinson's *Sergei Prokofiev: A Biography* (Boston: Northeastern University Press, 2002) and Laurel Fay's *Shostakovich: A Life* (New York: Oxford University Press, 2000).

Chapter 11: A Guide to America's Classical Greats

Leonard Bernstein's Young People's Concerts http://www.leonardbernstein.com/ypc.htm.

Aaron Green, "Popular U.S. Classical Composers," http://classicalmusic.about.com/od/20thcenturymusic/qt/Popular-U-S-Classical-Composers.htm.

Finale: A Guide to the Classical Future

Neumeyer, David, *The Music of Paul Hindemith* (New Haven: Yale University Press, 1986); Simms, Bryan R., *The Atonal Music of Arnold Schoenberg* (1908-1923 (New York: Oxford University Press, 2000).

Lisa Bernier, "9 Brilliant Contemporary Composers Who Prove Classical Music Isn't Dead," http://mic.com/articles/90713/9-brilliant-contemporary-composers-who-prove-classical-music-isn-t-dead, June 9, 2014.

Brian Wise and Naomi Lewin, "American Orchestras Grapple with Diversity," http://www.wqxr.org/#!/story/american-orchestras-grapple-diversity/, February 6, 2015.

"Just in: Report calls for 'equality quotas' in classical music," see: http://slippedisc.com/2015/02/just-in-report-calls-for-equality-quotas-in-classical-music/#sthash.yWYM-RJXr.dpuf.

Aaron Green, "5 Famous Asian Classical Composers," http://classicalmusic.about.com/od/biographies/tp/5-Famous-Asian-Classical-Composers.htm.

For a good synopsis of present and future trends in the expansion of the notion of what is classical music, see, *A History of Western Music*, 8th Edition, "Music since 1970," 970-86.

Bibliography

Abbate, Carolyn. *A History of Opera.* (New York: W.W. Norton & Company, 2012).

Abdul, Raoul. *Blacks in Classical Music, A Personal History.* (New York: Dodd, Mead & Company, 1977).

Alexander, Morin, ed. *Classical Music: Third Ear: The Essential Listening Companion.* (Milwaukee: Backbeat Books, 2002).

Berger, William. *NPR The Curious Listener's Guide to Opera.* (New York: Perigee Trade, 2002).

Bookspan, Martin. *101 Masterpieces of Music & Their Composers.* (New York: Dolphin Books,1964).

Copland, Aaron. *What to Listen for in Music,* Reissue. (New York: Signet, 2011).

Dubai, David. *The Essential Canon of Classical Music,* 1st Edition. (New York: North Point Press; 2003).

Goulding G., Phil. *Classical Music: The 50 Greatest Composers and Their 1,000 Greatest Works.* (New York: Ballantine Books, 2011).

Greenberg, Robert. *How to Listen to Great Music: A Guide to Its History, Culture, and Heart.* (New York: Penguin Books, 2011).

Jacobson, Julius H. II. *The Classical Music Experience.* (Sourcebooks, Naperville, Illinois, 2002).

Libbey, Ted. *The NPR Guide to Building a Classical CD Collection: The 350 Essential Works,* 2nd Edition. (New York: Workman Publishing Company, 1999).

Mordden, Ethan. *A Guide to Orchestral Music: The Handbook for Non-Musicians,* 1st Edition. (New York: Oxford University Press, 1986).

Pogue, David and Speck, Scott. *Classical Music for Dummies.* (New York: Wiley Publishing, 1997).

Rosen, Charles. *Sonata Forms,* Revised Edition. (New York: W.W. Norton & Company, 1988).

Rosen, Charles. *The Classical Style: Haydn, Mozart, Beethoven.* (New York: W.W. Norton & Co., 1998).

Ross, Alex. *The Rest Is Noise: Listening to the Twentieth Century.* (New York: Farrar, Straus and Giroux, 2007).

Rye, Matthew, ed. *1001 Classical Recordings You Must Hear Before You Die.* (New York: Universe Publishing, 2008).

Staines, Joe. *The Rough Guide to Classical Music,* Rev. Edition. (U.K.: Rough Guides, 5 Exp, 2010).

Steinberg, Michael. *The Symphony: A Listener's Guide,* Reprint Edition. (New York: Oxford University Press, 1998).

Swafford, Jan. *The Vintage Guide to Classical Music.* (New York: Vintage Books, 1992).

Veinus, Abraham. *The Concerto: From Its Origins to the Modern Era.* (New York: Dover Publications, 2012).

Watt, Robert Lee. *The Black Horn: The Story of Classi-*

cal French Hornist Robert Lee Watt. (New York: Rowman & Littlefield, 2014).

Index

A

B

C

D

E

F

G

H

I

J

O

P

Q

R

S

T

V

W

About the Author

Earl Ofari Hutchinson has an M.A. in Humanities from California State University, Dominguez Hills that included the Humanities course series on the advanced study of music, focusing on concepts of meaning and form in music. He is a sustaining member of the American Musicological Society. He has for a decade programed, featured and promoted classical music on the KPFK-Pacifica Radio Network.

From1995 to 2015, he attended nearly 500 concerts by nearly every nationally and internationally known major orchestra, and that featured many of the top virtuoso performers, and attended many major festivals including the Aspen, Bach Carmel, and the Ojai Festival. He has interviewed many of the leading classical conductors, composers, and performers, He has written about classical musical developments in his columns. He moderated the prestigious panel of classical artists and musicologists on the works of Dimitri Shostakovich. He has attended and participated in numerous concert lectures and preconcert lectures. He completed the Comprehensive Music Study Series based on The History of Western Music at West Los Angeles College and studied music theory and history at the Pasadena Conservatory of Music.

37064038R00161

Made in the USA
Middletown, DE
21 November 2016